From Blue to White
Quit Your J.O.B.

CHAD PETERSON

From Blue to White

Printed in the United States of America
ISBN: 978-0615893983

DEDICATION

To my loving son Cole, for being a silent motivator of success and greatness and for giving me the reason and opportunity to pass down my achievements.

From Blue to White

TABLE OF CONTENTS

ACKNOWLEDGMENTS

To all my readers who know they can win if they reach inside deep enough for the grit and gravel to push beyond normalcy to achieve freedom in their lives.

To my friends who have always believed in me.

To Kurt Hackman, there exists no other man I would rather walk with in life than you, brother.

A very special thanks to my friend and editor Alfie Thompson, without you this book would not have been born. Your drive and insight astounds me. Your ability to prepare a book for readers is wonderful and so is your friendship.

To my Mother, for without pressure diamonds cannot be formed.

To Orin Sweeney for being there.

Last but not least, for my late father: Your heart was as big as it was genuine; your laughter and charisma were contagious. You are so deeply missed and I long for your presence in my life. I wish you were here to know the man you never met in your son.

1

ME

I am a:

Hunter

Fisherman

Rock Climber

Body Builder

Skydiver

Snow Boarder

Commercial Pilot

Professional Underwater Diver

World Traveler

Collegiate Wrestler

Trained fighter

Serial Entrepreneur

Inventor

Life Coach

Business Consultant

Motorcyclist

Wildlife adventurist

Sailor

Explorer

In this career oriented world, people often ask, "What do you do?" I either answer "I am a contractor." or "I am in marketing." Either answer is a lie. What I do is varied and vast, and I am not defined by my occupation or how I earn my dollars.

What people who ask the question really want is a quick summary of who I am. We tend to find our box to put people in based, initially, on what they do for a living.

My true answer is that I *live* for a living. I don't work for a living. I am not one thing. I am many. I have many talents and abilities and a long list of things that I have done. My career choices pale in comparison to the diversity of my accomplishments and experiences.

If you also want to 'live' for a living, remove yourself from the kind of thinking that how you make your money defines you. Your life and how you live it defines you. Your job is for earning dollars. Dollars are the tools that afford you the experiences you will have and the type of life you will live.

Your life is much more than a job, your life is meant to be lived.

Time-Line

December 2nd 1978: I was born with pneumonia with a high chance of death at birth. I wasn't having it. Released from the hospital with a clean bill of health, ready for Christmas.

Lesson learned: I came into this world to win.

Spring 1980: I figured a way out of the house to go see what was out there in the big wide world. Found down the street in diapers, entertaining at a major intersection.

Lesson learned: Thinking outside the box is an adventure.

1981: I am now property in a custody dispute between a construction worker and a bar tender. Parents divorce. I'm already showing signs of quite a pedigree.

1982: Mom's second marriage is ending in another divorce.

Lesson learned: Something tells me it might be wise to be self sufficient.

1983: I'm enrolled LaPetite day care and don't want to be there. I hate naps. I want to build blocks but they're telling me to go to sleep. The next time they let me out to play, I escape. Kicked out of the day care permanently.

Lesson learned: Don't want something? Change it.

1985: Mom's marriage is again ending in divorce.

Lesson learned: Yep. Better figure out how to make it on my own.

Who knows what's going to happen next?

2nd Grade: Someone puts me on the wrong bus; the bus driver drops me off somewhere between I don't know where the hell I am and lost. I navigate my way home with the determination and the will of a man.

Lesson learned: I somehow know the cavalry isn't coming.

3rd Grade: Oops. I am in trouble at school for telling the teacher what she is teaching is stupid. I don't need to learn it. I refuse to do the work and I am sent to the principal's office. I nod my head and convince him that I am listening.

Lesson learned: I *think* he said that school was important.

4th grade: I see snow outside and grab a shovel. I knock on every door within walking distance and ask to shovel the driveway. Soon I have a game board box full of money at age 8. I want to earn $20 an hour so recruit my much stronger, older brother to help. I pay him $5 an hour.

Lesson learned: This self employment thing works.

5th grade: I begin mowing grass, earning $75 dollars a week. I have my eyes set on a new bike.

Lesson learned: Don't spend your money, 'Things' don't buy happiness.'

Junior High: I have a full blown lawn care company, complete with a vehicle of my own.

Lesson learned: School? A great place to go to see my friends.

High School: I make more than most of my teachers. I love travel and being a lake bum. Economics? History? Calculus? No thanks. I've already completed the necessary classes to graduate. I write a letter to the principle saying due to economic hardship in the home, I must work so I must be released by 10 AM to go to my job.

Lesson learned: Bullsh*t works.

1997: I graduate from High School, sell the business, drive off to college. My peers are anxious to join the fraternity life; not exactly my scene. I like being among the ladies. I pay them to take class notes for me and go bowling, drink beer with my buddies and fly planes. (Not while drinking, of course.) I ace the tests but discover there is no way I'm ever going to use this so called 'education.' I split and head to Florida for flight school.

Lesson learned: One must follow that quiet voice inside, the one whispering what is best for you.

2001: I am at a known flight school where Al Qaeda has several students training to fly planes.

I wasn't friends with them. I didn't know them. Don't look at me like that!

2002: I lose my job with an Airline, damn it. I kind of thought something was going to happen. I needed to do this on my own.

Lesson learned: Sometimes losing is winning.

2003: I open a mortgage company without knowing what a mortgage is, but business is booming.

2004: $4,000,000 in revenue.

2005: $6,000,000 in revenue.

2006: $5,000,000 in revenue.

2007: Too much. Too fast. 120 employees, 4 locations and not enough aspirin on the store shelves for my headaches. First lesson in management? Don't ever be in management. I shut down.

Lesson learned: When things are good SELL! I lost a company worth 8 million because I didn't sell it. The market changed and I didn't take action.

2008: I have been running a side business the past couple of years called Got Wood? a deck and fence refinishing company. I am an opportunist more than anything. I sell my business in 2008, ready for something new.

2009: I work for Orin Sweeney at Night and Day Construction. I develop marketing and sales directly for him and his multimillion dollar roofing and exterior company. I quickly learn the business. Soon I'm making a few hundred grand and working 6 months out of the year. That was working nicely. I trade that in for doing it all myself. WHY? We all fall prey to cultural standards of more, more, more.

Lesson learned: Less can be more.

2010: I am feeling like I did in 2007. It's time to reevaluate. Money vs. Lifestyle? I decide to make massive changes to my operation. I delegate to separate from the day to day operations and focus on what I am good at: business development. I add on multiple companies to my construction company.

Lesson learned: Balance can be achieved.

2012: One of my add-ons to my construction company is the largest concrete care company in the Midwest. Marketing is in place. Sales happen daily. My workers get the work done. Much of my time is spent with my son, writing, traveling, or on various hobbies.

I am 35 years old, semi-retired, I vacation anytime I want and enjoy my life as it was intended to be. I work to live, rather than live to work. I have created my life by design. I have made my life what I thought it should be and I am not under control from any outside forces. Nothing prevents me from living the way I want too.

This is my wish for you.

2

America

The land of opportunity. The promise this country held was awe inspiring. Our ancestors bit, scratched and tore to reach United States soil. Long boat rides with shortages of food got them across the ocean. They left family (our ancestors) behind for a new beginning and the incredible opportunity and promise that new beginning held.

The long train rides, the long journeys by oxen and buggies to find their place in this great country. And they worked hard and prospered.

America, the land of opportunity. This was our motto and creed full of strength and pride. To be an American was incredible, even 15 years ago.

Oh say do you still see strength and determination among the masses?

I sometimes think of the greats who built this wonderful country: Henry Ford, Thomas Jefferson, Rockefeller, Walt Disney, Thomas Edison, Alexander Graham Bell, the Wright brothers, Bill Gates and Steve Jobs, Oprah Winfrey, the list could go on and on. These forward thinkers knew one thing for certain:

no one was going to do it for them. They knew the cavalry wasn't coming to save them or to give them anything.

When you look around you today at Americans, do you see a nation of strong willed, opportunity thirsting, hard working people? People prepared to do what it takes to thrive and survive? I see few who have the gumption, the fortitude, and the hard working principles that built this country. Men and women of today seem to want everything to be done *for* them, rather than utilizing their given talents and their own hard work.

Knowledge—or the lack of it--is no longer an excuse to lean on. The lack of gumption, fortitude, audacity, and simply having the balls to get out there and try, to risk for the reward is a sure sign that with all the knowledge in the world, you still have to want to succeed to do it. The responsibility of reaching for success is yours alone. Without that, failure is certain. This shortage of the very principles that built this wonderful country is a cancer on the economic growth of our country. Excuses and unaccountability add to the doom and gloom of our current circumstance and removes any responsibility for solutions in this time of crisis.

The economic climate of the United States has never looked so hopeless. The debates amongst the powers-that-be, combined with few positive actions prolong and enable critical issues to further plague the country today. Unemployment rates are high, debt and spending has surpassed any in our history, and the declining morale of the American people has further created a congested economy. The debate rages on and on, but steps taken to remedy the situation are nonexistent.

The long list of excuses is getting much longer than the long list of problems. Is SOMEONE ELSE going to fix this? Is SOMEONE ELSE responsible for my well being? It seems that many believe that the problems in their lives and the economy are outside of themselves.

Entitlement Refined

Recently at the grocery store, I was standing at the cashier's, lost in my own thoughts and not paying much attention to the lack of movement in the line. When I finally noticed, the store checkout clerk was having a hard time with all of the government issued coupons and vouchers a young woman had presented. I thought to myself that it must be tough to have to do that. I bet it's embarrassing.

I then took a closer look. She had 3 kids grabbing at her and she couldn't have been more than 25 years old; she was on her cell phone discussing weekend plans with her friends; her nails were French manicured; she was dressed nicely for a mother of 3 using food stamps to buy her groceries. Her cell phone was--wouldn't you know it?--an iPhone.

My long wait in line was suddenly more disgusting. I was suddenly curious about her weekend plans. Did she have any intention of finding a job or perhaps creating one for herself? As I finally proceeded to check out, I saw a sign that said help wanted at the customer service counter. Was the young woman too busy on her phone and with her 3 kids to notice? Those of us who work and pay taxes were probably paying for the gas to get her to the store, the phone she was talking on, as well as the toilet paper she'd had in her shopping cart. I wondered when she got home, would she turn on her cable and watch her flat screen TV while she cooked her kid's dinner? Why would she search for a job if she can do nothing yet live well? The economy and the issues we face are complex. No one denies that. But at the end of the day, the solutions are simple. Work hard, exploit any talent you have, dedicate yourself to being successful at any cost. Help others along the way. Seeing you doing well may inspire someone else to do the same. An economy is really nothing short of people exchanging money. Money comes and money goes. This principle keeps the economy from being congested. With the flow of money from everyone, the economy would be back in full swing.

There are many books that promise to give you the knowledge to get rich or become self employed, or how to create an online job with little effort. This book will not promise to make you a millionaire (though some of you probably will achieve that—if you want it badly enough to work hard for it.) It won't make your life easy or magically turn you into an instant success. But I know without a doubt that hard work, consistency, and determination will bless your life and remedy the issues that create an America that looks like yesterday's, instead of the country we see today.

A Country Restricted

As the economy has failed, the government has put Band-Aids over hatchet wounds. They've bailed out corporations that need help to survive. They've enabled a society that lacks accountability and responsibility. If you are reading this, you are probably a hard working individual looking for a road tested map to master the steps to become self employed in a working trade. Homes across the country are in need of valuable services. Too few providers exist to supply those services, and most don't know how to get out there and win the business. Once they do, many don't know how to facilitate the work.

As further government regulation hits so many industries, the profit margins become slimmer than ever. Many business owners' hands are tied as government control becomes out of control. Contrary to politicians' well written speeches, jobs are NOT created by government. Jobs are created by those who possess the entrepreneurial spirit who want to create a life for themselves and others. Home service based businesses have less risk and less chance of failure than businesses that require a large amount of investment in over head and debt to get started. Meanwhile, millions of customers wait on valuable service providers to do quality work at a reasonable price to keep their homes in good condition. I will point you in the direction to get there, to get work and become a broker of services to others. I will show you how to be the professional who knows how to market and create demand for high paying services--if you are willing to work for it.

The books that will tell you how get rich quick without effort have already been written; the ones that promise a world of instant success with little effort have also been written. No book will help anyone succeed overnight or become a millionaire easily.

You must make the decision within yourself to be the best that YOU can be. The army may have used it for their tag line, but the truth is that you *can* be the best that YOU can be—and that is your benchmark to live by.

We all grow and push beyond our previous limitations to reach new heights. I believe the need to do so was written in our hearts; that we must move forward and accelerate to new accomplishments or something within us dies.

This book was written to give you practical steps and ideas on achieving your personal best.

3

Adventures in Entrepreneurship

I am no different than you. We are the same. I don't have any more ability or talent than you. I doubt I am smarter than you. I certainly started with no money, and I have had little support from outside sources. Not a source to help me borrow money. Not even good advice.

When you hear success stories, do you dismiss them, believing, "It was easy to do for him because _____ (Insert reason here)?"

I can honestly and boldly tell you I came from nothing and started with a little less than that many years ago. You currently have the resources and enough money to start your own business. There is no excuse you can use for a crutch.

What you are going to learn, I learned through years of hard lessons of trial and error. Your cost—the price of this book--is minimal compared to the more than two million you will earn if you apply my methods, and will afford you something even more valuable than money; your **freedom**. If you apply what I teach you and utilize the resources I've put together, the coaching, the business mentors and the online communities full of resources, you will make more than a few million dollars in your lifetime.

Opportunity is all around you. You just have to know how to capitalize on it and follow through. That is what you will learn here.

This is not a gimmick to get rich quick. There is no such thing as get rich quick, or an easy path. I am not selling multi level marketing or a strategic way to make money using creative tiers or fad theories. Nothing here is designed to instantly change your life. However, if you put the work in, I have a road tested, battle-worthy plan for you to put in place with little money. It offers an escape from the grip of corporate American Slavery or the J.O.B.

I will ensure your success if you let me.

I don't have a rag to riches story to awe you with. I don't have an AHA! Moment to share. No light bulb went off in my head and changed something deep inside me to send my career in this direction. My passion to become a success can't be attributed to anything heroic or courageous.

I was phobic of the idea of working for someone else or in a corporate system until I could *one day* finally retire to enjoy my life. Work now--enjoy later? Didn't work for me. That was never an option or goal of mine.

The thought of working my entire life under someone else's business plan frightened me. I wanted to enjoy my life now; I wanted to experience freedom now. Besides, who ever said the boss I would work for was doing things right anyway? I didn't want to make someone else money and watch myself get tired with an over-worked mind. Not for the greater good of the company or the boss.

If my back was going to get tired or my mind was going to be worn out, it was going to be for me: Chad Incorporated.

"One day" dreams of having enough money or time or freedom was too many days away. I wasn't going to spend a minute investing in another's vision.

I never had the mindset of an hourly employee. I didn't look for jobs that paid an hourly wage. I did not want to be on someone else's clock. If you told me right now that I have to stay somewhere for a certain period of time and that if I leave, I will not be paid, I would leave now. Keep the pay.

Put me on a clock and I feel imprisoned. I'm literally phobic of the idea.

Rather than being on a clock and seeking jobs that paid by the hour or a fixed salary, I focused on the game of how much money could I make with no help from anyone but me.

How could I go out and make money and stay completely independent and self sufficient? How could I make 5 times as much money in half the time as I would working for someone else?

Embracing the Entrepreneurial Spirit

When I was young I would knock on doors and ask if I could walk the neighbor's dogs for $5. When it snowed I shoveled driveways for $40. When I was a bit older, I began mowing lawns. When I learned a bit more, I began to offer lawn treatments and to fertilize lawns. With each new account I added to my schedule, I earned a measly $35 a week more. But those $35 jobs added up quickly.

By the time I was 18, I was making more than many of my teachers. I remember looking at them, watching them do their best to teach me all they could, and thinking that I had already figured out what I needed to know. I knew how to be independent, successful and the captain of my own ship. Tapping my foot and bored to death I barely made it through school. Learning algebraic equations and about our founding fathers, government and sociology became painful.

As my foot tapped, I waited for the bell to ring so I could get out to the real world and earn my living. I was able to afford a brand new truck and expensive equipment for my business. I had more freedom as a 17 year old kid than most grown men have today.

I made $3,000 a month working for myself, part time back then. I was a teenager with a pocket full of money, no one clocking me in or out, and nowhere to be at a certain time. I was completely in charge of my schedule and my life at all times.

The teachers didn't know how to do what I did; my peers didn't either. Many of my friends worked long hours at a car wash and made fairly decent money. But they wore clothes they didn't want to wear and had schedules that demanded that they be there at whatever hour their boss commanded. Night or day. Day or night. It affected their school and their social life.

I couldn't have done what they did if I had too. I made 10 times more money in half the time and still had time off to go to the lake. I had hobbies and personal time. I wasn't chained to a system or anchored to the clock.

If I needed something, I bought it. If I wanted something I could get it and not worry. Money was coming in faster than I could spend it.

A Brush with 'Real' Jobs

The only 'real job' I was ever interested in having was as a Firefighter or an Airline Pilot. At 19 I went to take the test to become a firefighter… and failed. I called the testing center and they referred me to the national testing company who did the test. "How could I have failed that test?" I asked in dismay. "It was easy!" The reason for my failure, they explained, was that I was deemed "Unmanageable."

At first I was indignant. "What? That's crazy! How can they say that?"

The test asked questions like: What tool would work best in this scenario?' There was a picture of a nail and you were to pick between a pair of pliers, a hammer, a pair of safety goggles. Easy. What I didn't know was that the questions were also asking me about certain scenarios because it was a psychological test. I failed to fit the psychological profile to become a firefighter.

I was deeply disappointed. I knew that as a firefighter, I could still run my business on my days off and what little boy doesn't want to ride in the big fire truck?

When I told this story to friends and others, they would laugh. Immediately. They were all amused that

I didn't know this about me. Come to find out, they were also laughing at my surprise. Was I the only one who needed a test to point out that I was unmanageable?

I have come to like that story.

As I've grown older I couldn't agree more. If I had to sit in a fire station for 2 days knowing that I wasn't getting paid anymore than my salary I would go crazy. I would sit and watch the clock and feel like I was wasting time. The clock would be ticking opportunity away.

I decided to sell my lawn and landscape business and go to flight school.

I was able to sell my company for a year's revenue and go pursue my dream. I packed up and drove to Florida to attend a well-known flight school in Orlando.

I spent over $140,000 on flight school and flight time. Living on income from the sale of my business and a window cleaning business I started when I got to Florida, I was able to get through flight school with minimal student loans. I became a Commercial Pilot at the age of 21. It was July of 2001.

Everyone knows where they were that awful day in September when the Twin Towers were attacked and fell. I remember it perhaps even a bit more clearly.

I was piloting a plane, 20 minutes Northwest of Orlando International. (Coincidentally, that is where President George W. Bush and Air Force One were at the time.)

When I was told to land immediately, my only guess was that someone feared Air Force One would be attacked and they were prompted to take drastic measures.

The Florida skies are the busiest in the country and Florida has more airports and runways than any other state for its size. The skies were full and the runway was about to be packed with a traffic jam.

Coming in to land, the tower asked all pilots to point the nose of the airplane at the runway and turn on the lights. (It was broad daylight, mid-morning.) The sky lit with the lights of hundreds of planes, all coming to the same place: one runway they wanted us all to land on immediately.

It was scary. Sweat poured down my face. I was a nervous wreck, getting that plane down in this very strange scenario. It was intense. I landed the plane right after another plane, another one landed right behind me. It was a very high paced clearing of the sky, not only where I was, but throughout the country. And it was especially intense where the President was.

I landed safely, loosened my tie and walked to the briefing room where TVs were showing the coverage of that awful terrorist attack that changed the world. Over 100 pilots were in that room, knowing that the career we wanted had just come to a screeching halt. I held on and stayed optimistic that the Airlines would still be hiring at the rate they were prior to the attacks, but the truth was soon revealed. After all I had worked for, all my hard hours in ground school, studying and testing; all my efforts were for nothing. I felt robbed and cheated.

Beginning Again

The Airlines stopped hiring all together. Airlines struggled. Travel as we knew it was changing and so was my life. When I learned I also had a surprise baby on the way, my dreams of flying for an Airline became a distant memory.

Struggling with depression, the upset, moving back to Kansas City from Florida, my dreams turned to becoming a father and picking up where I left off.

I got back into town, still in shock that I was not going to fly a plane and travel the world.

In the early 2000s, the mortgage business was big and many were doing well in it. I didn't know what I was going to do for a job, but I knew that many of my friends were making money in mortgages. I decided to learn.

I went to a friend to learn the business and began to sell mortgages for a local operation. Within 3 months, I had earned 30K and in usual fashion I decided that I could do it myself. So I did.

In 2003, I opened a mortgage brokering company with one employee for less than $5,000. By 2005, I had 120 employees and 4 locations across the Midwest and my company was generating over 4 million a year in revenue. Keep in mind, I hardly knew anything about mortgages; I just knew how to build and operate a business and I hired accordingly. It wasn't easy. I fought for success and stayed focused until I hit my goal: I exceeded 5 million in revenue in 2005.

I then opened up a title company, figuring I might as well make the additional money from every mortgage my company wrote, rather than someone else.

Again, I knew nothing about the title business. But again I did know how to open a business and get systems in place. And I already had the marketing issue figured out. The mortgage company was doing 100s of loans a month; the title company was passive, easy income.

I thought my gravy train had biscuit wheels and we

were never going to see the end come. I was wrong. As heavy regulation came in and changed the industry, I failed to see the writing on the wall. My business was worth over 8 million dollars and I literally let it rot on the vine.

A lesson I will never have to re-learn. When things are great, SELL!

I shut down the company and was back to **"now what?"**

Although it was a haunting and aggravating scenario at that time in my life, it was a wonderful time for me to regroup and switch gears.

I had worn a flight uniform and then a suit and tie. I decided I wanted to lose the attire and get outside. I wanted to feel the sun and get out of the office. I began looking for the kind of opportunities that are always around us.

I was asking, "What can I do and make good money at it? What is something lots of people need?" I began to notice decks and fences in the neighborhood. They were being left untreated and turning grey and black. They were not being maintained. They were ugly and becoming eye sores.

I went to the hardware stores to learn the process of beautifying a deck or fence from start to finish. I started on my own deck. And completely failed.

This failure was the start of my learning. I learned that not only were the decks and fences in my city falling down and rotting away, the store you visited to learn how fix the problem might not tell you how to do it correctly!

I began to research different methods of taking an old fence or deck and making it look new again. My research gave birth to the new company, "Got Wood?"

I bought a power washer, the chemicals I needed, an assortment of paint brushes and a paint sprayer.

Before I knew it I was bringing in $30,000 a month. I added vans and vehicle wraps to my operation and made a marketing impression on Kansas City, resulting in the largest deck and fence refinishing company in the area.

After 3 years, I did what I SHOULD have done when things were great with the mortgage company. I sold it. Apex Business Solutions was able to sell my business fast and for a good price.

I sold for a reduced price of $150,000 since I just wanted to move on to the next thing and take my experience to new levels.

Making 25-35K a month for 3 years, selling the business for $150,000 with only a few grand invested…I was all smiles.

But as Apex was presenting me with buyers—though the buyer pool was slim--I was hard pressed to find the right candidate.

I wanted someone who was hungry to buy the business, someone who wanted to win, wanted to fight for success, someone who was willing to learn. The right buyer came. His name was Keith. Keith was an engineer who sat in a cubicle solving math problems and creating engineering diagrams. Throughout his career, he had never seen outside of his cubicle or his computer. He had never been in sales, didn't know the first thing about marketing or operating a business. He was green as green could be and I loved it.

I knew that if I could train *this* guy to do what I did, I would be able to teach anybody. He was teachable; he didn't fight the process or try to do it better; he simply followed what I taught him and nothing else. He purchased the company from me and I taught him from the ground up, just like I am about to teach you.

Be Keith

Now, I ask you to be Keith. Don't question or challenge me. Do not dismiss what I am saying. Open up and allow me to teach you what I know. Have faith in me and yourself. Know that I know how to help you fire your boss and become your own boss. Let me help you make your own money--as much of it as you want.

I have the knowledge to help you create the life you want. A life of freedom, both from money worries and with your time. Freedom, money, and pride in what you do. I will free you of the regular work schedules, inadequate lunch hours and clocking in and out to work a mundane job every day.

You don't have to do that anymore. You are holding this book because something in your gut says, "I can do it." Something says, "I want better." Keith, the current owner of Got Wood? is still doing well. He and I have become friends. With my help, he is now franchising his business across the country. I have taken an engineer who knew nothing about business to being the head of a corporation bringing in 100s of thousands a year. I can help you do the same.

4

The J.O.B.
Just Over Broke

Market Panic: Time to be Self Employed

If you have paid any attention to the news lately, you know the unemployment rates are as high as they have been since the Great Depression. The question media moguls ask is "How will the government fix the problem of unemployment?"

I'm not an economist, but I have the answer: Stop giving away free money, put a stop to the handout nation and people will be forced to flourish all on their own.

The Handout Nation is today's cultural epidemic; suffocating the human spirit. The epidemic pacifies and enables those who want a free ride and allows them stay unemployed while their bills are paid, groceries are bought, car payments are made, and cell phones are free. All courtesy of Government handouts, paid for by U.S. taxpayers. Those who take advantage of this ask themselves an entirely different question about the job market. Why get out there and work for a living if I don't have too?

The government initiated failure rots our economy from within. When there are more people looking for jobs than there are employers looking to hire, it puts everyone in the position of becoming part of the Handout Nation. To avoid that, if you want to survive and thrive, you have to make it on your own by using these tough economic times to your advantage. That was how our country was founded and it worked well until our government got too big to let economic growth happen.

It's time to reset, to get back to basics, and make it for ourselves. Entrepreneurs like yourself, pursuing the dream of prosperity, rather than waiting for someone to do it for you, are the key to rebuilding our nation.

Yesterdays Answer: Education

Let's reverse 30 years. Education was valued and something to immerse yourself in if you wanted to be marketable to employers. Education institutions across the country were offering more and more courses of study and an ever widening variety of degrees. The job market was booming, and the baby boomer generation catapulted college degrees to the new standard for employment. The line of applicants was short and the number of applicants standing in that line with degrees was even shorter. The chances of finding a job were great if you held a degree, showing the competency to make it through 4 years of commitment just after high school. The belief was that if you could make a commitment to yourself to do something voluntarily like make it through the university; you were a great job candidate.

Fast forward to today: EVERYONE HAS A DEGREE. There is a reason that colleges are now marketing for new students today more than ever. The advantage a degree once gave you is now a formality. Just like everything else over the last 30 years, education has become big business. The hype that "if I have a degree, I will get a good job and become successful," has saturated the job market with long lines of degree holding applicants that too also bought into the belief. The advantage is gone. Job applicants have a hard time differentiating themselves from other candidates. By and large, 'higher' education is waste of money and time unless there is a burning desire to work in a specific industry that requires 'higher learning' such as being an attorney, a chemical engineer, doctor, or dentist.

Over 80% of college graduates don't have any idea what they want to do with their degree. I hear students say "I am going to get a general degree that can be used for anything." I can't think of a more wasteful use of $100,000 and 4 years of life. It's time to start thinking about how you can open new doors and become independently successful and free of the employment machine.

When is the last time you heard someone with a job say "I have plenty of money and time at my disposal?" or "My employer is paying me too much; this job is so great I don't understand why they pay me?" My guess is you haven't ever heard either of those things.

I bet you have heard, "I work my ass off and can barely make ends meet." Or possibly, "The office wants me to work overtime this weekend. Weekends are a thing of the past." The reason is simple: *that's how it was designed.*

The employer (soon to be you) strives to conduct business at the lowest cost possible to maximize profit. Labor and salaries can be a broken and bleeding artery in a corporation if not carefully checked. They ultimately can be the death of the company.

So is it a surprise, corporations aren't handing out wages that allow their employees to soar higher than

JUST.OVER.BROKE? (Or the acronym: J.O.B.) For all intents and purposes, you can apply for any job and when asked to insert your desired salary, just write just over broke on that line. It is what you will get anyway.

If an employer pays much more than that, he or she will soon be looking for a J.O.B.

Too much month at the end of the money is the syndrome most deal with in homes across the country and in our government itself. The U.S.A. is running on a negative bank roll. Debt has become the norm and a J.O.B. will not get you out of it.

Jobs traps are endless. Chase more hours to earn more money, more shifts and hopefully a promotion. Seldom do those things meet our expectations, much less allow personal freedom for the lifestyle you really crave. Time spent away from the home increases, retirement income decreases, quality of life decreases as the pressure of the so called "horrible economy" increases and affects the country's strength and morale.

In the movie **Jerry McGuire**, Tom Cruise (as Jerry McGuire) talks to a little boy on a couch after having way too many cocktails. He starts spewing his hatred for corporate America to a 4 year old boy. "My Dad worked for a company for 40 years!" he tells the kid.

"And the only thing he complained about was that he could have had a more comfortable chair!"

In his half drunk dialogue to the boy, Jerry realizes he is seeking reassurance from a 4 year old that his point is valid.

His point *was* valid. A company used to take care of its people. Now it's about how much can you get out of the employee or how little the employee can do in order to keep his or her job. The employee/employer relationship has deteriorated the last 20 years. The belief that a company will take care of you, value you and support you has shattered. Tighter markets and smaller profit margins have reduced profits while new companies saturated the market with growth it couldn't sustain.

But there is good news. You no longer need an employer for your security. You can have it all on your own.

Times have changed

For years, companies offered jobs because they had the real estate to facilitate having employees. For all intents and purposes, you needed the company for their resources. Internet wasn't available, cell technology unheard of. Today's technology--instant messages, fax via emails, cell phones, the internet— have made it possible for home offices to be as well equipped as a company with a big building and limitless office machines. All the knowledge and information at our fingertips, plus ways to market online and every tool imaginable is available to YOU. The employer isn't holding the only golden egg anymore; you can easily be just as equipped to conduct business as a large company. Combine the changes in the market and the availability of resources, with the eye opening truth that companies aren't employee focused or concerned about your well being or your long term career; it's time to start looking at YOU INCORPORATED.

Whether you work in an office or are a laborer, you can become your own master today and walk away from the collar and leash of Corporate America. You can put your hammer down and employ others to hold the hammer. You can shed the tool belt and sweat and be in charge of the others who will do the work. You can be independent, have your time and your freedom and be limited by nothing.

It's time to start thinking about how you can open new doors and become independently successful and free of the employment machine.

Freedom is yours if you believe that you can do it. Are you ready to be free from corporate chaos and be your own master?

It's all about Efficiency

If there is one thing lacking in corporate America, the work force in general, and our government, it is efficiency.

Employers spend most of their time and money preventing problems, preventing law suits, preventing sexual harassment, preventing the competition from knowing what they are doing, conducting time sapping, grueling meetings and training, defining protocol and policies, putting in place checks and balances than they do producing the goods or services that provide their profits. The "Machine" becomes slow moving, inefficient, and less profitable. The cost of doing business skyrockets as the corporation becomes riddled with protocol, process, and red tape. As my Dad used to say, "Son, sawing saw dust is a waste of time; just make sure you are finding new boards to cut". He was referring to not wasting time analyzing what you did rather than focusing on what you need to do.

As the soon to be self-employed master of your own destiny and prosperity, you have the ability to create your own efficiency to make the best of your days. You can accomplish your dreams as you see them. The quickest way between two points is a straight line. This book is your straight line. It is designed to get you to the destination you have in mind, quickly and efficiently. Efficiency will help you maximize your profit and income and will also increase your quality of life.

Money vs. Life style

This is *not* about becoming rich. Money comes and goes, but we have one shot in this life and it's how you live it that will determine if you feel it's a life well lived or a life wasted. For all intents and purposes, money only makes you happy if your bills are paid and you have your basic needs met. A little bit of money in the bank is gravy. It brings ease. An excess of money doesn't create happiness.

I have made millions and wasn't any happier with that money than when I had $5000 in the bank. The life style one lives determines happiness.

For me, happiness is not being on a clock or scheduled or even managed. I would last 2 days if I had to deal with a job like that.

Most of this book was written while visiting Central and South America, traveling and seeing the world. Money is freedom and the lifestyle I have created by not choosing a traditional job has proven its worth time and time again. I don't have to bite my tongue and deal with an employer. I feel like a billionaire if I have my bills paid with no one to answer to. Lifestyle and freedom is far more important to me than money or monetary success. The knowledge I'm going to give you will supply you with both the money and the lifestyle you want, and as much of it as you want.

I only work from March through November. I am done working for the year on my birthday on December 2nd and my birthday present to myself is travel abroad. From the principles I'm going to show you, I am able to leave the United States for 3 months or more, see the world, taste new food, experience new cultures, and literally be retired for 25% of the year. I have seen most of the world. I plan on seeing it all.

If someone asks what I do, I tell them, "I am in construction." When you think of someone who is able to travel like that, do you think of someone who has been working for 40 years, retired, and has a pension? Or do you think of the CEO of a company who works remotely and lets his company run itself? Or do you think of someone like me who works in construction?

I'm a 35 year old man who started my business with less than $2,000. I have turned it into a million dollar a year business working from March through November and I have designed my life to be free of the chains of corporate America. I am not one of the walking blind, thinking that one day I will enjoy my life and do the things I want to do. I do it now.

I am no smarter than you. I don't have special abilities. I'm a regular guy from modest roots, born and raised in the Midwest. I never bought into the pipe dream of the J.O.B. My goal was not to work all my life to one day relax and retire.

Call me impatient. Call my lifestyle instant gratification. Call it what you want. I call it freedom. And you can have it too.

Gut-Check

I've put down Corporate America and the J.O.B. a lot so I want to say a few things about employees, as well.

The vast majority of employees grumble about things like "If I owned this company I would sure do

_____ differently." or "Damn company is doing this all wrong," under their breathe, complaining and griping throughout their working years. Does it somehow make their life better?, Does complaining about a job, even knowing you aren't ever going quit or make a change help? Are you going to do it yourself? Or is it just bitching to bitch?

Let the fear of not being successful dissipate for a moment. It's time for your moment of truth.

ARE YOU READY?

Are you ready to be your own boss? Are you ready to get up in the morning and fight like a lion to make it happen? Are you ready to make no excuses and find solutions? Are you ready to feel like you are going to make it against all odds? Are you ready to realize you only have one shot and you must do well in order to be successful?

If your answer is yes, that is far more important than the knowledge of HOW-TO do it. The world is inundated with knowledge. At the click of a button you can learn anything from making bombs to doing brain surgery. You can Google and find the answers. But the real answer lies within you. Are you really ready to live your dreams? Are you really ready to have freedom? Are you really ready to not have a boss? Are you really ready to make the money you deserve? Are you really ready to take that vacation you always wanted to take?

If you are truly ready and willing, that is the hardest part. We can do the rest together.

5

Why Blue Collar?

Take a look at the housing boom over the last 30 years. The growth has been phenomenal. For a decade, there weren't enough hours in the day or enough lumber to build as many houses as the market demanded.

The growth opened an enormous market for qualified service related businesses across the country. All of those houses were not built maintenance free. And in most cases, the house were built as fast as could be; resulting in future problems for the eventual homeowner.

The vast majority of new home buyers have no idea that maintaining a house costs as much as it does. Because of the mortgage boom, low interest rates and creative financing programs, many bought their houses with nothing down and were house poor from the start.

The houses needed maintenance they couldn't afford. The homeowners needed someone to do it. Homeowners didn't know how to hold a paintbrush;

they didn't know how to fix a deck; they didn't know how to lift fallen concrete; they didn't know how to install windows and doors or carpet; they didn't want to clean windows or know how to roof their house or fix their plumbing.

The good news is that you, the soon to be service provider, doesn't need to know how to do any of that either. Homeowners are spending more time working in the machine of Corporate America and less time at home. When they *are* home, they don't want to work on the house. So the avenues are wide open because the number of contractors, service providers and entrepreneurs offering these services, pale in comparison to the need.

While this economy is less than desirable right now, a home must still be in good condition to sell it. And because of the poor economy, far more people are looking to upgrade their home rather than buy bigger. They want to maintain and beautify the one they have.

As the housing market shows some signs of improvement, the need for service providers will increase. Right now, there are simply not enough to meet the demand.

Yesterday's Man

How many men do you know who can use a hammer or fix a minor leaky faucet? How many men do you know personally who would get out on their deck to power wash and stain it themselves? How many are willing to get on a ladder and paint their own home? When was the last time you saw a home owner trimming tree branches? Do you often see a homeowner bringing in rock and mulch with a Bobcat and doing heavy landscaping?

Most homeowners will spend thousands of dollars before they take on a project themselves. The handyman has become a dinosaur. By and large, homeowners hire out what they need have done to maintain their homes. In some parts of the country, it is rare to see a homeowner even mowing their own lawn. Ninety-five percent of the things people used to do themselves are hired out today.

Technology- The Erosion of Man

The future generations of men are today's little boys in 3rd grade classrooms using laptops. They already know how to use Microsoft Word and how to search the internet. They are the video game generation. Is that generation of men going to be wooing a woman with their handy-dandy fix-it skills? I don't see it happening.

Technology has pushed our youngsters away from labor and hard work. Everything is instant: instant email, instant gratification, instantly look up the current score of the big game you can't attend on your phone. The video game, technology generation is certain to make the handy husband extinct.

Technology may allow men to keep track of projects for work, to manage data, to run an entire corporation from a laptop, but the knowledge, skills and abilities men once learned from their fathers have eroded. The gap between projects needing done and qualified workers able to do them is growing.

There exists an enormous market for you to start your own home service business and the future will only make it larger. The techie generation may not even know how to mop their own floors. The market is vast and is growing.

Why from Blue to White?

It is time for Blue Collar workers to put down their tools and become the guy who goes and gets the business, the guy who manages the projects. It's time for that guy to be paid the lion's share of the project. On the other hand, if you currently work in an office and would like to escape, there is a very narrow margin of successful corporate start-ups. Perhaps you should consider venturing out into the Blue Collar service related world.

I could just as easily have named this book From White to Blue. I am not specifically targeting the working man, or even just men. Many women make 100k incomes a year supplying services to individuals and enjoy all the freedom they want.

Those who are tired of the suit and tie and want to feel real sun rays on their face instead of artificial UV office bulbs; those ones who are fed up with the pressures at work, worry about increasing layoffs and uncertainty in the market in general; those staring at a computer screen all day bringing home the same pay week after week, year after year with little promise of anything changing from day to week to year, including their quality of life; those who are ready to manage themselves and call their own shots and create their own destiny; those who are tired of getting to work at 7 AM and coming home at 6 PM; those sweating for $12 an hour while his boss makes $300 an hour: this wonderful opportunity to learn from the ground up how to offer a service related business and earn in excess of $100,000 a year starts now. Listen up.

I own multiple blue collar related businesses. Blue to White is about becoming self employed in Blue Collar service related fields. This is not about turning a mechanic into a millionaire; it is not about easily using your skill sets to make money doing everything yourself. I'm going to show you how to be at the top of the food chain in a service related business, regardless of your current skills. Never been in a service related field? Never even worked with tools? No problem. You can make six figures, starting today with no experience.

If you are currently a concrete finisher and you want to go into concrete finishing for yourself and make 50% more by cutting out the boss, the information you need is here. If you don't know a thing about trade related services, this book is for you. If you want to go into another field and leave your current skill set behind, that works too. In most cases I can teach you how to run a business in a trade or service that you know nothing about. I aim to prepare you for success no matter what your current skill set.

The Demand

Homeowners in your neighborhood have needs that are not being met. Many of the things they need don't have any licensing requirements.

Lawnmowing

Powerwashing

Landscaping

House Painting

Housecleaning

Concrete Repair

Concrete Lifting or Mud Jacking

Deck and Fence Repair

Deck and Fence Staining and Refinishing

Sprinkler System Installation and Maintenance

Tree Trimming

Tree Removal

Window Cleaning

Window Installation

Wood Rot Repair

Door Repair

Door Installation

Foundation Repair

Roofing

Insurance Related Hail or Storm Damage Work

Siding Installation

Gutters and Drainage

Concrete Finishing

Garage Organization

Deck Building

Fence Building

Carpet Installation

Carpet Cleaning

Granite and Other Types of Countertops

Remodeling

Packing and Moving services

Christmas Light Hanging

Snow Shoveling

Insulation and Energy Efficiency Improvement

Stucco Repair

Drywall

Outdoor Living Space Design and Construction

Concrete Staining and Sealing

I could go on. The demand is high. The supply of providers is low. Furthermore, the business skills of those who offer the services are often inadequate. They do not know how to capitalize on the opportunities that lie directly in front of them.

All of that information is your ace in the hole, the feather in your cap. Service providers don't know what I'm going to teach you. That is your saving grace. They may know how to do the work, but they don't know how to get the work and manage the business end of providing those services. They don't know how to grab the volume of business they want and if they do obtain large volumes of business, they often struggle to manage the work load.

Armed with my knowledge, you will soon be better equipped for building your business than the competition. You will learn to bring in more business and do it faster and more efficiently. Stay beside me and you will learn how to do all of this. You will be successful.

Considerations

The service related businesses listed can all be started today with little capital and zero tools. Yes, I said it. You can start any of the above businesses with no experience, little or no money and no tools. We will get into the details shortly, but for now, consider a few factors in choosing what service you wish to provide. Do not let negative self talk interfere. "I don't know how to paint houses." "I don't have the tools to fix decks." You know those thoughts that were passing through your mind as you read the list. You don't need experience or tools or knowledge. What you need to consider is what you *think* you would be interested in doing.

What do you see yourself working on?

Would you rather offer painting services or landscaping?

Would you like to get into roofing and storm damage restoration?

Don't choose your service related business based on what you know now or what you have on hand to start the business today. Rather assume you have all the knowledge, skill, and tools to do any of those services. Starting today. Don't let fear get in your way. By the time you finish reading this book, you will know how to operate any service related business.

6

Goals, Reasons and Timelines

I haven't met you. I will most likely never meet you. But I know you. I know the "You" that you've always wanted to be.

The person reading this book believes in himself. The person who bought this book aspires for more than he or she has today. The person who stared at the cover trying to decide whether to buy, or spent time researching the book online was in a zone. He or she saw opportunity, waiting to be unleashed if only he or she had the right answers.

You have a burning desire. You want it all and you want it now. You know that within you, there exists an unlimited force that will stop at nothing to grasp your dreams.

Life and the world throws more and more at you, distracting you from reaching the success you've always known you could have. What you want is very real and obstacles seem to crop up in the just the right way, at just at the right time to always divert you from your goals. You are very frustrated.

Some people don't try to be successful or live on their own terms. Others don't know how to tap into their full potential and exploit it. Most wannabe successes have not had the right teachers or mentors. They lack real and usable advice buried in the endless ocean of information in our technological saturated world. More than anything, most dreamers have not been successful because they never really ask themselves what they want.

Sounds easy, doesn't it? But if you haven't soul searched and really seen what you want in life, it can be very difficult to achieve anything.

I Bet You Don't

Though it should be an easy task to sit down and write out what you want, it may be one of the most challenging things you have ever done.

At first blush, you think you know your goals. Do you know your goals and desires? Sit down, think about it, and write it out. What do you *really* want? What *are* your goals for yourself? Not as easy as you thought, right?

But define your goals and then allow yourself to learn. (I have trained staff ready and willing to help you in your journey if you find any of the steps I'm going to share with you, too daunting.)

Now define all the reasons *why* you want what you want. Goals without reasons are pipe dreams and have no purpose. Pipe dreams never come true. Authentic emotions drive a person to a goal.

For example, if you say, "I want to be a multi-millionaire," but have no emotional reason behind the goal, you won't provide the force behind the action that will help you achieve the goal, and most people don't ask themselves the WHY. You need the 'why' to follow through on that goal. It is a must and it is more important than the goal itself.

Goals without timelines are open ended statements, incomplete sentences, a watch without an hour hand: completely worthless. When thinking about your goals, your reasons why and the timeline you will put on that goal, it must go in that order. You must feel and believe that the goal is obtainable and you must see them as though they are already true.

From the time you have your goal (and its reasons and timeline) in mind, you are no longer allowed to say, "One day I will _____." That type of goal setting is for those who won't reach their goals.

When is one day? And who says you will be around "one day?" You must live as though your life is today. Tomorrow may never come. Each day is a gift. Maximize your time and efforts because today *is* your life.

Begin by planning your goals in small segments of time. You can progressively set goals for further out as you lay it all out on paper.

The first few steps are the hardest and usually require the most energy. If you wisely set very short term goals, you'll find reasons for small celebrations along the way. Start with a 30 day plan, a 60 day plan, a 90 day plan, then step it up to 6 months. Then plan for a year, then 2 years.

Anything farther out than 2 years is a waste. You and your business will evolve. Projects take on a life of their own. I am usually presented with so many more options in two years that I have to go back to the drawing board and reset my goals higher than I originally dreamed they should be. One thing is sure: if you discover what you want and the reasons why, the emotional anchors--the burning desire, you'll be unstoppable in reaching your goals in the time you have determined you'll reach them.

7

Brokering of Services

Being self employed comes with a heightened state of awareness that *you* must provide the service at the right price to a customer. But did you know that over 90% of business is brokered? One entity contracts to provide service, another entity fulfills the work to provide the service.

Think about your cell phone provider. Does your cell company put towers across the country? Are they the ones who warranty your phone and fix it if it breaks? The answer is no. It is all brokered. Cell phone companies market the services and rely on others to fulfill the needs. They deliver a good logo, a memorable tag line or message to the public, set a competitive rate structure, heavily market the services and then hire other companies to fulfill the orders.

The term broker has taken a beating over the years. However, even large corporations broker their products and services. The label on your shirt is not the company making the shirt. The soup in your soup can is not the company that made the soup. The brand on your shoes is not the company that made the shoes.

For most, this concept is an eye opener. We should all know this, but we don't. (At least consciously.) What products do we actually make in the United States? I know very few off hand; we outsource or broker everything.

How about mortgages? From 1990 to 2005 over 95% of mortgages were done through brokers. Lenders and banks knew the volume was too much to handle in house, so they created a way to use brokers. They offered services and sold those services through brokers across the country, that's the only way they could keep up with the high demand. Millions of mortgages were sold, but only a small percentage of them were actually done through the bank itself. Once your mortgage was complete, it may have been sold 2 or 3 times before it ended up with your current lender. Many people were part of that transaction, but it was the mortgage broker who did the marketing to obtain the client. The name of the actual service provider or bank (lender) came later.

Auto manufacturers opened brokerages (Dealers) for their products. They knew the marketing (and access) had to be done nationwide at the local customer level, not from the factory. Dealerships were service centers and offered warranties and repair. It took thousands of dealerships across the country to fulfill the high demand for vehicles. If you drive a Chevrolet, how many people were "brokered" to get your car in your possession? Let's look closer at this.

You looked through the paper to find the car you wanted. (The newspaper was 'brokered' to market for them.) If you called the phone number on the ad on a Saturday, chances are an answering service was 'brokered' to pick up and asked if they could help you. You go to the dealership yourself and look at cars and a sales man earnestly greeted you. Once you decide on a car, you go to the finance office where the dealership has aligned themselves with various banks to offer you financing. (The financing is brokered.) The finance manager offers you an extended warranty plan (which is brokered). The salesman may have signed you up for XM satellite radio and/or on board GPS and road side assistance. (All brokered). Insurance is also brokered through an insurance company. By the time you buy that vehicle, up to ten people, working for companies other than the manufacturer have been outsourced to make the sale happen.

Keep this concept in mind, know it and understand it is YOUR model as a new service related business owner.

In operating your service based business, you don't have to be the master at whatever service you are offering. Do not put that pressure on yourself! You simply have to be good at 'brokering' services and following through to make sure the job gets done and gets done right.

Look at any building, whether it is a sky scraper or an elementary school. A large general contractor was hired to build the project, but the contractor himself did not know, and never will know, the entire scope of work needed in order to build that building. From the grading of the ground and the preparation of the site, to the foundation, to walls, to electrical work, to plumbing, to the roof and the locks on the doors, the general contractor found providers for each piece or part of the work. He picked the best company to do the best work for the best price to maximize his profit. There are a million ways to make a million dollars. You just have to pick one and do it well. You don't have to be the marketer, secretary, order filler *and* the service provider all in one. You just have to know how to market and broker those services.

Brokering of services is simply this: You obtain a client. You effectively meet that client's needs through another party. You are paid to be the middle man. This is how things get done. Businesses outsource their work to direct employees for fulfillment or they contract with an independent 3rd party. Anymore, almost all customer service is 3rd party. Very few services provided today are *not* brokered.

The most important thing you need to know right now is that you don't have to be good at everything (or even anything except matching service providers with those who need the services) in order to be self employed. You will essentially broker out your labor, your organizational skills, your accounting, your legal, your secretarial work, your assistant and perhaps even customer follow up and your drip campaign marketing.

Master the idea that all you have to know is how to broker services and be profitable at it. The one thing you need to be good at is marketing your new business that you are about to open.

We are in a brokering world where marketing is the most desirable and sought after skill to master. Fulfilling the work or providing the product is the easy part.

8

10 Steps to Get You Started

Step 1- Open your Business

The simplest way to get your business open and ready to do business is to form a Limited Liability Corporation or LLC. An LLC is less cumbersome and regulated than a corporation. You won't have a heavier tax responsibility than a larger corporation would under more traditional forms of corporations. As an LLC, the money earned is taxed once. Typically, the LLC owner is sheltered from other tax implications that come with other forms of corporations. LLCs allow the owner to shelter himself from business liabilities and debts if they occur.

For now, open and operate your business as an LLC unless your accountant tells you otherwise. As you grow and begin to earn more than $500,000 annually, your accountant may suggest you change the structure. But for now, an LLC is the easiest way to get started.

At this point, the name of the LLC should NOT be the name of the company. This may sound strange, but simply put, the name of your company does not have to be the same as the name of your business. I own many companies but my corporate tax filing is different from the name of my business. This allows flexibility in the future if you want to add services or market an entirely different service. If you were to name your company Residential Solutions, for example, you might find it hard to market your company name to a commercial entity. The name of my LLC is Peterson Companies, LLC. Under that corporation I operate many LLCs, 'doing business as' (or DBA) whatever other names I use for those companies.

Filing your LLC need not be difficult. The LLC doesn't need to say what you do or even the name of your business. It is simply a corporation, owned by you, and you can operate as any business under that limited liability corporation.

Keep it simple and name it *your last name,* LLC. Or name it a word you like. How about Synergy Worx, LLC.

I recommend using www.llcaction.com. This company can help you with the paperwork you need for filing in any state. They will check if the name you choose is available, they will file your corporation with the state, they will also provide you with an operating agreement, file for your Tax ID number, file for your letter of good standing, and get you all of the documents you need in order to go to the bank and open your business checking account.

Once you determine your business name and create your LLC (www.llcaction.com), you can then leave it open to file any DBA or fictitious name and you can begin to operate as such.

Step 2 – Get ready for Money

Go to the bank with all of your documents from www.llcaction.com and open a business checking account. Be sure to open your account with a bank that is small business friendly yet has the technology to communicate with Quick books accounting software. This is crucial. It will save you time and money. Let the bank know that you will be operating as a DBA in the very near future. (If you know at this point what the business name is, put that name on the account, too. Banks know how to do this simple thing and can easily do it now or later.

Order a debit/credit card with your company name on it and order your business checks with your LLC name on the checks. Order carbonless copy checks. This will be invaluable in keeping records of your expenses. (It will also aid your accountant when doing your books at the end of the year.)

Now, you have opened a business, formed an LLC and opened a checking account.

But you may not even know what you will be doing. Seems crazy, doesn't it? I assure you, it's not. Follow step by step. You will get where you want to go soon enough.

Step 3-Discovery

If you don't know what service your new business will provide yet, it is time to research the various avenues. Are you going into the same line of work you are currently because it is easy for you since you already know it? Or do you want to find something new? Something more profitable?

What you do today doesn't mean you can't do something else tomorrow, if it means more profit and a lifestyle that more accurately matches your desires. What services are needed in your area? What do you see around you that needs improved or enhanced? What service or product does your area lack that you could provide?

Start watching your neighborhood and city for what is needed. Are fences and decks looking shoddy? Is everyone's landscape a mess? Are there an ample number of cleaning services in your area? Are the cleaning or maid services struggling for business because they don't know how to market? Do you see lots of dead limbs in the trees when you drive through neighborhoods around you? What is obviously needed?

Ask questions? Find out what service homeowners or even businesses have trouble finding. Check several months of your local newspaper's classifieds. Is there anything that is needed and showing up consistently? Stay away from 'trade' oriented things such as electrical or plumbing service. It isn't that you *can't* open a business providing that, but you'll have a lot more headaches. And for the most part, that type of business won't bring in more profit to make up for more headaches. Unregulated, labor related services can be marketed with little or no red tape or licensing requirements, which isn't necessarily true of trade oriented services.

As you get closer to deciding the services you want to provide, it is time to research whether or not you need a license. Do you have to take a test to get it? If you know the service you intend to market, you also need to do a little competitive market research. Get bids from other companies who offer the same service or a similar one. What are they charging? Simply call the soon-to-be- competition. Get a quote or estimate.

Let's say you are thinking of a house cleaning service. Do what other consumers do. Get 3 bids from local companies. Besides finding out prices, watch how they present their company, what sales points they make, and how they make their presentation.

Maybe you're interested in house painting. How do the painters you get estimates from charge? What makes their company different than others? Ask the guy who gives you an estimate why. On everything. I call this "Contractor Espionage." Interrogate him, become a sponge, take notes. How will you do it differently? How can you make it better?

Spend a few nights on your computer discovering various services you can offer. Find prices if you can. The price tag for most services offered will help you determine your bottom line. What are the margins? What kind of profit can you expect?

We will get into margins and profits later, but begin to learn your trade or service and understand the margins allowed to keep you competitive. What will your materials and labor cost? Can you offer multiple services? Consider all options during your discovery process. Limit yourself by nothing. All options are open. And if you need help, we are here for you. Do you need advice or coaching? Do you need to consult with someone who can give you good advice and point you in the right direction? I have coaching resources available on my website: www.bluetowhite.com/coaching.

Step 4- Name your Company

The name of your company is important. It may be one of the most important things you do at this stage of your business. Many things come into play with the name you choose. Besides saying what you do, it should be obvious what you offer. It should be well thought out in order to stand out from the crowd and you *do* want to make a name for yourself.

I started a Deck and Fence Refinishing company and named it GOT WOOD? It was a play on the "GOT MILK?" advertising that was popular at the time. The principle behind the name in this case was that it asked a question that resulted in a 'yes.'

A homeowner seeing GOT WOOD? Deck and Fence Beautifying and my phone number answered 'yes' and the name of the company said exactly what I did.

They get the message in an instant. No guessing. The subtle sexual innuendo in the name of the company didn't hurt either. Compare that with some of the names of my competitors. Father and Son Painting, Advantage Deck Care, or Resilient Deck Care. Guess whose name customers remembered?

(These companies all started after I had started mine. I was the first one in the area to offer this service and the competitors came flooding in.)

The name of my company stuck, it was more powerful, simple, and had a touch of humor in it. Combined with the "Got Milk?" ad campaigns, it was memorable time and time again. As immature as it sounds, the sexual innuendo made it even better. It worked.

I can't tell you how many housewives would comment on the name. It became a topic of conversation around town. "Hey, have you seen that big white van driving down the road with a vehicle wrap that says GOT WOOD?" Often, we'd be stopped at a stop light and people in cars around us would be snickering. I wasn't laughing when I deposited over $250,000 in my new business back account my first year in business.

If you think you may want to grow into other services, you also want to keep this in mind. If you want to start a house painting service but you plan to extend your services to commercial painting eventually, you wouldn't want to name your company "_____ Home Painters, Inc. would you? Think ahead. Think of your target market and name your company accordingly. The name must reflect what you do quickly and be catchy so that people think about it for a minute. When you drive down the road and see a personalized plate and can't figure out what it means, do you find yourself sitting there trying to piece it together. Ten minutes later, after the car is long gone, when you finally get it, you feel like you just won at Wheel of Fortune.

This is the same principle. This is where your name is burned into their mind. You want people to see your company name and think about it. You want them knowing and thinking about it. You want it to permeate their mind and if the number has what you do in it as well, that is even better. 913-231-DECK. GOTWOOD? Deck and Fence Beautifying. 913-231-DECK. The branding and name recognition will help them remember the number and all together, it begins to build your name.

Your business name is also important if you plan to market online. If your name doesn't say what you do, the search engines won't recognize or find you.

If I offer concrete tear out and replacement, what is the likelihood that I will get a concrete tear out and replacement job if my website is www.petersonconstructionandroofing.com? Even though concrete replacement may be offered at my website, the search engines—if they recognize it—will place it on page 327 of the Google search. How often do you click on page two or three of a search? I for one don't go beyond the first page. I stand a greater chance of getting business from my website if I name my company www.concretereplacementkansascity.com.

Do you want your customers to consider you a big company? Name it accordingly. You can't market yourself effectively as a large company if your name is Bob's Painting Service. If you name it Legacy Painting with subtext that says, Your Complete Residential and Commercial Painting Solutions," chances are, people will think 'large.'

Keep these things in mind when naming your company. As soon as you have a name, make sure you file your DBA with your bank and other appropriate places.

Step 5- Develop Your Company's Wardrobe

What does your company look like? What is its image? What colors do you envision? Branding is important. The image and presentation of your company is crucial in winning sales over your competitors. You must look the part. Your company must look the part. And all materials such as your business cards, website, pamphlets, handouts, agreements, bid sheets, shirts, hats, etc., should have your 'look' and brand. Simply put, your 'look' and brand will create the image that you are legit. Your company knows what you are doing. Perception is everything. By the time you finish this book and complete the steps, you will look and talk like you have been in your business for 25 years.

Have your company's image created by a graphic designer. Work with him or her until your company image is just the way you want it. If you need assistance we have proven, reliable graphic designers and resources available through our website. We will help you in any way we can.

Step 6- Develop Your Presentation

The success or failure of your business depends on your presentation to your customers. The branding--

the business cards, shirts, website, etc.--show the look and feel of your company, but how you present the service makes the sale.

How you organize yourself and your bids and presentation is very important.

There may be 10 different ways to organize and present your services. I'm going to share with you the one I have successfully used for over 10 years. It keeps me organized and my sales presentations effective.

I don't use technology--laptops, email estimates, new aged gadgets or apps--to present my services or provide bids. I find that a 3 part carbonless copy is the best and most simple way to conduct your business and stay organized.

(There are examples of the fronts and backs several agreements I have used for various companies and services in the appendix of this book.)

Carbonless copies make it so easy to manage your business. Initially present the homeowner with the top sheet of the 3 part carbonless copy. The front should have your company logo, your contact info, and fill in the blank lines and spaces for pricing the various aspects of the services you will provide.

The back of the agreement will have the terms of the agreement, legal and informative items about your services and should address their expectations about what you are doing for them. Once the homeowner is satisfied that you will be the one to do the work they need, you must have them sign the agreement and provide them with the top or white copy. (Again, have this designed by your graphic designer so that it is sharp and presentable.)

Step 7- Organize and Follow up

Buy the kind of 9-pocket folder you can find at Office Max or Office Depot. They are the divided plastic style organization folders that have kept my very *unorganized* self, organized and on top of my work load, day in and day out for over a decade.

In the first pocket, you'll want to keep your blank agreements.

My 2nd pocket is labeled RV, for Residential Visits. The next pocket is labeled WARM. After I have met with a prospective customer and given them my presentation and an estimate or bid, I may not yet have closed the client on the service. I need to follow up with them.

The next pocket in the folder is labeled CLOSED. They've signed the contract for service and the signed contract goes in this pocket.

The next several pockets are used for the each step in your service. If you are a house painter this pocket may say Clean, meaning you are ready to power wash the house.

The next pocket may say Prep and the next folder may read Paint.

The next pocket will say Complete meaning you are done; you've finished with the job. You need to settle up with the client.

My next pocket says OOPS. That means there is still something that needs to be done. For a painter, it might mean you need to touch up, clean up, or do minor touch ups for the client before you can collect.

The next one says MONEY. File all your checks in this pocket as you receive them from your clients.

The next one says CLOSED OUT. The job is done. The client has paid and you are finished with that job for good.

This organizational system keeps you knowing where you are with each client, each step of the way. It is fail proof; it doesn't rely on technology, battery power, access to the internet or anything else. It easily sits beside you in the seat of your car, everywhere you go. You are aware and always knowledgeable about every job, every step of the way.

The top copy of your 3 part carbonless agreement

goes to the homeowner. The middle and 3rd copy stay together in the WARM or CLOSED pocket, wherever a client is during the sales stage.

Your hired labor will probably need the details and the information about the job so you simply give him the middle or 3rd copy. You keep one for yourself and it will progress each stage to completion until it is filed in the COMPLETE pocket.

Knowing how much money you are bringing in may lead to resentment or entitlement setting in with your laborers. If this is a concern, simply fold back the 3rd page of the agreement when you fill out the money details of the job. Then be sure to give the crew or laborers that part of the agreement. This is your call, of course. Does your hired help need to know the price tags on the work being done?

The 3 part NCR (no carbon required) agreement and the 9 pocket folder will keep you organized and able to manage a large volume of business without having to spend a lot of time doing paperwork or entering data into a spreadsheet on your laptop to stay on top of things. This is easy and flows wonderfully on a day to day basis. There is always time later to convert your information into Excel or another database.

Step 8- Find Your Help

I've said several times that you don't need to know the trade or service that you are going to provide. Here is the secret revealed: *your help does.*

Our economy is in such a state that there are more service professionals out of work in all the trades than there are qualified entrepreneurs to provide the workers with work. This is your power as an entrepreneur.

I can teach you how to build a business, to market, to sell and to organize. I can show you how to keep the lion's share of the money earned. You are going to let a professional, who has been doing the trade you are offering for most of his life, handle the work.

If you launch a painting company, do you need to know how to paint well? Do you need to know how to mask off and prep the walls? Do you need to invest in ladders and all the equipment? No you don't. You need to find the business and contract for the labor. Let them, the professionals, actually handle the work. You are a broker of services. Sound crazy? It's not. This is how the world works.

Do football coaches know how to play football better than the players? Does the owner of a major food chain know how to cook as well as the people they hire to do it? Do record executives know how to sing as beautifully as recording artists they give contracts to? No, all they have to know how to do is find the talent and give them a platform or the opportunity to show their expertise.

Just for grins and giggles, get on your local craigslist and place this ad:

Experienced Painters Needed ASAP

$12 an hour starting. Respond, only if you have experience and all the tools needed to be ready for work. We are painting homes; you must have a lot of experience painting homes and ability to prove your experience. Professional painters only, please. Respond with your telephone number and your availability to work immediately.

Do not put your phone number in the ad unless you want to listen to it ring, non-stop all day long and into the night. Have them respond by email so that you can get back to them at your convenience. This is a great way to find your painters (or any other professional service provider). Talk to those who respond. Talk to them about how they paint, how they prep, what steps they take, the equipment they have, how tall their ladders are, etc. Let them educate you. If you plan to go into the painting business, keep the ad running. You will quickly have 50 painters at your disposal at any time. I have ads running at all times for every trade. I can offer any service possible at any time with professionals in each trade. You don't need full time employees, you need professionals who are good at what they do and want the work. You are providing them with a service they need. You know how to get the business. They don't or they wouldn't be depending on craigslist (and you) to find jobs. This will work in any industry or trade. Right now, there are more workers looking for work than ever. Capitalize on it. Pay only what you need to get qualified help. Maximize your profits.

Step 9- Clout and Recognition

Web Presence

At one time during the dot.com revolution, a company was legit or established only if they had a website. It took money, programmers and designers to make that happen. You had to have a nice site that looked the part.

Today for $12 (or less) you can buy a domain name and a template that needs minor alterations for $60. In no time, you are online.

Just being online will not bring you business. Now days, having a website without massive marketing is like having a beautiful home in Egypt. It might be spectacular and well built, but are your friends going to come see it?

The time your website has been established, how well it is built, ad words, Meta tags, social media, tweets, and search engine optimization play a part in your website's performance. You don't *need* to have a website to receive business. If you want one, just know that you will not receive business from it unless you use the many resources available in order to make the website visible to the search engines. For all intents and purposes, a website only suggests that you are established and gives your customers something to look at if they wish. This could aid in helping you seem well established to those who believe having a website makes you legit.

The only purpose at this point is saying you have one. It is similar to having a degree if nearly everyone has one. What is the value? Same with websites. Everyone has one…you won't stand out by having one, too.

If you plan on having a website, there are plenty of options when looking for a website design and marketing company, but there is one clear choice if you are looking for a quality site at an affordable price. Hippo Daddy Web Design consistently sets itself apart from the competition because they work for your business by offering sample sites before you pay one penny. They don't offer empty promises...they deliver real results. (You can find their contact information at www.bluetowhite.com.) Once you become a client, Hippo Daddy supports and guides you through the complex launch and SEO (Search Engine Optimization) process for exposure. They make every site from scratch and are experts in online marketing, viral marketing, and SEO.

The BBB and Angie's List

This may surprise you, but I will never pay to belong to the BBB or subscribe to Angie's List.

I have made millions of dollars and have never paid for any reporting service to provide me clout or recognition. Simply put, it's a racket and a waste of money. The BBB has convinced millions of businesses that they need to pay $300 a year or more for them to 'recognize' you.

Wouldn't you love to own a business that made millions of other businesses pay $300+ a year so they would say they 'approved' you? The truth is, if someone wants to complain about your business, they can whether you pay or not. Why pay for their "accreditation?"

Clients can also go online to forums and complaint oriented websites, Facebook, and other social media and complain virally.

You can lose your good name in an instant if you don't take care of your clients and provide the service you say you will. Paying for approval is snake oil. Many law suits are placed with the BBB and Angie's list because of vindictive homeowners who want to destroy a company if they feel they didn't receive what they thought they were going to get or perhaps they want things for free. Other times their expectations are out of line. If they have a legitimate complaint, fix the problem.

Times Have Changed

Go about building clout another way: Social media. Facebook (and other social media outlets) is the new age reporting system. With the new viral technology, you can promote your business rapidly and get 1000s of likes and testimonials in a short period of time or over the life of your business. Comparatively, the BBB reports only negative feedback and doesn't promote or talk about what you do or how satisfied people are with your service.

If clients ask, explain why you don't belong to the Better Business Bureau. Tell them to check your Facebook page or look up your online reviews. Ask them to 'like' you and leave comments or possibly review your business after you complete the work for them.

There are other ways to create clout and recognition. Networking groups put you in an environment where others are willing to share business with you and be a mouth piece for you if you do the same for them. This is a win-win. Join a networking group or establish contact with other business owners whose services compliment yours. You'll be amazed at how much business those 'friendships' can bring.

Step 10- Prepare for Battle

You are going to war. This is a fight. You will be out there hunting and battling. Get prepared. Do your homework on the trade you offer. Do your due diligence on costs and know your pricing structure, based on your labor costs. Know what your materials will cost. Know how much money this is going to take to get started. If you think it's going to cost $2000, plan on $2500. Be prepared to be the best at presenting what you do. Know the business. Ask your new-found help questions. Ask about every aspect you can think of.

If you are going to pour concrete, know enough to teach others. If you plan to offer housecleaning, know what hot buttons to push to sell your services. If your company is going to do landscaping, know which flowers must have sun and which can thrive in shade. Know what each costs, as well as the cost of mulch and rock. Become a pro. Have your labor ready. Get ready for battle.

This is war and you need every weapon available and ready.

9

Compensation

One question I always get when I am coaching new business owners is how I do payroll. Paying yourself and others can be a daunting task. It's hard to do if you have never done it.

Most of the time, your accountant will guide you. Most accountants can do payroll for you and get the proper documentation from federal and state entities for taxation purposes. They can also assist in doing the 1099's for your contract help.

1099 help or employees?

Do you want employees and the tax implications that come with 'employing' them? Or do you want contract labor? The difference? With employees, you have to take out their tax liabilities and pay things like Social Security taxes and Worker's Compensation. The government attempts to prevent paying help as contract labor from time to time, but those attempts have so far, fallen short. With Contract Labor, you are not your laborers' employer. They, like you, are self-employed. You send them a 1099 at the end of the year. They are responsible for their own taxes.

There are advantages of both. As contract labor, being self employed allows your contractors to write off expenses such as gas, cell phone and equipment. As employees, your help will have fewer hassles with paperwork and taxes, but they will pay more. You will also pay more by the time you add in the additional taxes and paperwork.

The contract labor route usually saves both the employer and the laborer taxes. Some accountants recommend that you require your contract labor to have an LLC and a Federal ID number to ensure you have no problems later. Others don't think it matters. I usually pay each Friday and write checks for labor performed that week directly to my help as 1099 contractors. I never pay the labor costs until I have been paid for the job. If you pay people early, or before the job is complete, you may never see the job finished and be left with a problem to fix. Make sure you are paid first as the service provider; then pay your help.

At the end of the year I send out 1099s through my accountant so I can justify all my expenditures for labor and contract employees. The contract employees ultimately need their own accountant to file their self-employment taxes.

There are other options available. You can hire a payroll service or another contract laborer to come in for only the hours required to do your payroll and withdraw taxes from checks and file them with the state and federal to ensure proper taxation.

How do I get paid?

One of the advantages of being self employed is that almost everywhere you go your expenditures are on the company. If I fill the tank on my truck, pay a cell phone bill, buy lunch for me and my crew, buy work boots or shirts, put tires on my vehicle, pay insurance on my vehicles or put one in the shop for an oil change or repairs, the company pays the bills. If you don't have a lot of additional expense, you don't have to draw a big salary. I pay myself the same weekly pay check as I pay my contract labor. On Friday, when I'm paying bills, I determine the amount to pay myself based on the week we had. A good week with high revenues? I pay myself more. If it was a lousy week, I will pay myself less. The flexibility is one of the things I love about being self employed. Being paid based on how hard you work rather than because this particular amount is what you get no matter what you do, is definitely a perk and great personal incentive.

It's all yours in the end

At the end of the year, after I take my small weekly salary to pay my personal bills while the company pays for my expenses, my accountant tells me how much money the company earned for the year. That is how much I earned.

Taxes are based only on what is left after paying all the expenses. Though it may look like I brought in $700,000 in revenue, contract labor, employees, truck, tires, oil changes, advertising, cards, shirts, gas, equipment, and a business trip (and vacation), lunches, dinners, office supplies, miles driven are deducted from that. What's left is taxable income. That's the amount I pay taxes on. If I can show expenses and loss to bring my income down to $50,000, it's like living a 6 figure lifestyle yet being taxed on an average salary. I would have it no other way.

Most of the money you will be taxed on will come in at the end of the year. Profit is almost invisible until then. It's a matter of cash flow.

You must respect the money in your business account as such. As the business owner, you must use the funds in the account to keep the business running. It's wise to have the mindset that what is in the account is NOT yours, but rather the company's money. However, when everything does catch up, it's all yours. In other words, I have paid my help, I have spent all the money on materials I've spent all the money on materials and advertising for the year that I am going to spend; all my expenditures are paid. Say I do 20 jobs this month and the final half of each job is due 10 days after billing. By the time that money comes in, I have 30 more jobs that I've already paid labor, materials, advertising and all the operating expenses on. By the time I've been paid for those 30 jobs, I've done and paid for another 40. And that's how it works until the end of the season, when things start slowing down and everything catches up. My money (profit) isn't seen until the end. Cash flow is very important in a service related business. This compounds and compounds until the very end of the year when things are slowing down, the money rolls in and finally, all the bills have been kept paid and I see money for myself. When you hear someone say he has cash flow problems, it doesn't mean he doesn't have money; it means he doesn't have the money yet.

Get a good accountant, be aggressive on write offs and be sure to take the maximum write offs the tax rules allow. This country was built on entrepreneurship and tax law is written and designed to help you grow your business. Make sure your accountant is behind you on this and wants to minimize your taxation and maximize your profit.

10

Debunking Myths

Myth #1: You have to have money to start a business.

You have enough money to start a business. I don't know your financial situation, but I do know you have enough money to start a business in a blue collar field. Sure, the fear of starting your own company would be minimal if you had lots of money in reserve. But often, starting with nothing leads to the biggest success; you know you have to succeed because you don't have much choice. Money in the bank reduces the stakes and the risk and definitely reduces the motivation and dedication. If the only currency you have is motivation and dedication, it is worth far more than dollars in the bank. All effort pointed towards your business and a balls-to-the-wall attitude will help you win. You won't win, you won't succeed without it.

Myth #2: The majority of new businesses fail.

50% of all new businesses fail in the first year. So that makes the myth right. Right?

Wrong. Lack of resources, poor planning, inadequate market research, lack of dedication and follow through are the reasons businesses fail. The majority of new businesses fail because not enough thought goes into starting them in the first place.

The number one cause of a business's failure is lack of common sense. Let me explain. You live in a town of 5000 people and love making pizza. You have worked in the pizza parlors in town and think you can make a better pizza so you borrow the money from family or qualify for a SBA loan for $60,000 and open up Mickey's Pizza Palace.

The gumption, planning, and over the top enthusiasm for your new business will not help you if you haven't considered the one major fact that will make you a success or break you: there are 5000 people in your town. Most of those 5000 may eat pizza once every 3 weeks. With 3 pizza places to choose from, your sales possibilities are limited from the start. Soon you are bankrupt. Just because you make a mean pizza doesn't mean you will be good at running your business or good at marketing. Common sense would tell you that you don't need make a good pizza to run a pizza place. But you'd better be a good marketer and business owner to sell pizzas to the public.

You see gas prices going up and up and decide there is a hole in the market. You open a motorized scooter store because at 135 miles per gallon, there will soon be a demand for scooters. People will want to save at the pump. Your business plan proves on paper that buying a scooter makes complete sense. A perfect business plan, gumption and proof that your customers will have daily savings on gas will not trump common sense. Very few people will give up their cars and trucks. No matter how expensive gas gets, cars will be driving down the road. People may carpool. They may work from home a few days a week. They may find a job closer to home. You aren't going to single-handedly change the way people travel.

You make great smoothies so you sign an $8,000 a month storefront lease in a prime location. Your smoothies cost 50 cents to make. At $3.50 each, you will have to sell a minimum of 533 smoothies a week, just to pay the rent. That doesn't include labor, utilities, advertising, the cups to put the smoothies in or any profit for you. Have you investigated the average traffic in your area each day? How many people work close by? Where is your closest competition?

Most businesses fail from lack of common sense. Being an entrepreneur who makes good pies, makes awesome pizza or knits fantastic sweaters doesn't mean that you can run a profitable business.

Nothing in the information I'm giving you is gimmicky. The philosophies are tested, tried and true, as well as being practical and usable. Your business will not fail if you prepare properly (using common sense). The marketing techniques, pricing strategies and information on how to run your business are time tested. There are additional resources available on our website. Using the philosophies I'm presenting will provide the lifestyle and money you desire.

Myth #3: It's all about word-of–mouth.

People communicate through devices today. Do people actually talk anymore? When is the last time you had an uninterrupted talk with someone without the demands of daily life interrupting? And text or email communication may be part of those demands? Has anyone told you lately of a good service provider that you should call? Did someone refer you to the company that changes the oil in your car? Have you heard of a house painter who is really good? How about lawn mowing or landscaping service? Has anyone told you your yard will look great if you just call _____? I'll almost bet the answer is no.

Word of mouth is dead. People don't talk. Times have changed. People who once sat out on the porch and talked to the neighbors have disappeared.

Many will tell you the success of your business depends on word of mouth and referrals. I'll tell you that no one has the time for it anymore. Our fast paced lives and cultural movement towards technology communication force us to communicate through Facebook and text messages. Real conversation is dead.

If you start a business, understand that word of mouth is not the way you will get customers. If I relied on word of mouth for my businesses, I would not be sharing my success with you. I would be bankrupt and peddling the myth that "it's all about referrals and word of mouth."

In a given year, out of the 1000 jobs my various businesses do, roughly 0% of them are from word of mouth or referral.

It is what it is. Be aware of it and get used to it.

We are in a marketing world. (See Chapter 11) Plan on constantly marketing if you want your business to thrive.

Myth #4: You have to know accounting to be self employed.

This one thing scares off many hungry entrepreneurs. You would be shocked at how many people never start a business because they are fearful of this. I know nothing about accounting besides how to take my bank statements and receipts to an accountant I trust. He spent the better part of a decade learning how to number crunch. Not only do I not know about accounting, I have zero desire to learn anything about accounting. The only thing you need to know is how to regularly make deposits, pay your help, and pay for your operational costs. Give your bank statements to your accountant and let him do the rest.

You needn't write down every mile you drive or every meal you have while doing business. You don't need to carry a suitcase size bag of receipts for everything you buy. Simply pay for everything with your business debit card and take your bank statements to your accountant every 3 months. Let him do your taxes as well as your financial planning.

These professionals offer easy ways to shelter yourself from tax liability and maximize your overall profitability. Trust them; don't get caught up in the details. Find a trustworthy CPA to guide you through and provide advice, as necessary. If you give the accountant a full look at what you do, he will guide you in maximizing legitimate write offs and expenses and help you keep your revenue.

If you operate a service related trade business and are hiring knowledgeable experts who know how to paint houses, pour concrete, landscape, build decks, clean, mud jack, etc., why wouldn't you also hire an accountant who knows how to do what you don't?

If business owners needed to know accounting to open a business, only accountants could own businesses. ***Delegate at all costs.***

Let accountants and financial planners be experts at what they do; you be an expert at what you do.

Myth #5: It's hard to be self employed.

Typically, working for someone else, you are up at 6 AM. You commute to somewhere so you can be told what to do. You will spend 414 hours in traffic coming to and from work or 10.5 working weeks sitting in your car to make it to work and back home in a given year.

The harder you work, the same pay comes in; reward for your hard work comes in the form of simply keeping your job. THAT seems hard.

You do it all for time cards, deadlines, and a fraction of the pay you could be earning if you knew how to do it yourself and did it. You may get one week paid vacation a year so you can go somewhere and decompress. After a year of working 40 hours a week, you will have worked 2,080 working hours of your 4,160 waking hours.

Because of the current economy, your job is most likely no more secure than the average self-employed persons'. And the market changes constantly. Anything can change at any time with your job. The unemployment line is much longer than the line of self employed people looking for a job.

If you can master the book's techniques, your life will be much, much easier and without the trials of working for someone else. You may work hard, maybe even harder than you've ever worked for someone else, but the rewards are far greater, even with the added responsibility. And the potential for even greater rewards is limitless.

Myth #6: You have to be passionate about what you do.

I used to think I had to be passionate about what I did if I wanted to make it my career. I stayed true to this until reality was too painful to bear. The truth is we all want to do something exciting and fulfilling. We all want to do something that feels like it is what we not only want to do, but are supposed to do.

I remember wanting to work with sea lions in the zoo. I remember wanting to pilot planes for an airline. I remember wanting to be an astronaut. Somewhere along the way, I realized my goal shouldn't be doing something fun or exciting for a living. My goal should be to live a balanced life and having plenty of time to go, see, and do all the things I ever wanted to do.

I am a pilot, a scuba diver, a traveler, a motor cyclist. I ride bicycles. I go white water rafting. I camp, horseback ride, swim and go to beaches around the world. I do many things I love. I do what pays me enough money to afford a life style that includes all of that.

I literally don't work for 3 months a year. I have a mini-retirement every single year. If I was living in corporate misery, I would surely give it all up and be homeless. I can't work daily, day after day, year after year after year with little reward or change. I need long breaks and 'me' time.

Movie star? Celebrity? Porn star or garbage man? It all gets boring eventually. A job is a job, no matter how you cut it. Doing only what you love—whether self-employed or working for someone else, may lead you straight to failure. What if you love what no one wants or is willing to pay for?

Admittedly, I would love to have had Tom Cruise's career. Yes, I'll take Donald Trump's, too. I would love to have been on the ship that discovered the Titanic. But I know I can do exactly what this book teaches and make more than 6 figures a year and design my life just how I want it to be.

If your business idea is driven by passion, use common sense to take your passion to the market and earn money doing whatever it is.

Myth #7 People need jobs. I can hire good help to build my business.

Ok, get used to it. YOU are the only one who can make your business succeed. Yes, there are plenty of people out of work. More than ever in my lifetime, but not all of them want to work. Many are not forward thinkers who, like you, want to be self employed and find ways to get things done faster, more economically or better and with few costs and problems. That is your mindset. Good luck finding someone with that same outlook. It is hard, if not impossible to find.

Yes, there are millions of people out of work. However, with today's handout nation, who needs to work? We have a nation of unemployed who are talking on personal cell phones paid for by taxpayers, watching big screen TVs and not looking for jobs. They are waiting on the government to pay their bills. You will find more of these employees than you will the ones who want to help you take your business to the top. No one will dedicate his life to you and your dreams. It just is what it is.

From this point forward, know that employees are just that--employees. If you think you can reform them to think like you, you are wasting your time.

Your role is serving you well. Don't worry about trying to find another you. It won't happen.

Be the one who is makes it happen. Be the one you can count on. Others are going to do what they need to do in order to get through their day with their J.O.B. attitude. Forewarned is forearmed.

Myth #8: You must follow a business plan.

I would be one hell of a business plan writer if actually I sat down to write one. But I never have and I doubt I ever will. I would love to see the statistics on the number of failed businesses that started with impeccable business plans.

A banker once asked me to put one together to present to his group so they could determine if I could borrow $60,000 as if what I put on paper was going to predict the future; ultimately assuring them that this was fail proof. That was when I first started my self-employment journey years ago. The banker said my business plan wasn't complete or sufficient enough to get funding. I took my tax returns back to him recently and said, "It looks like my plan worked. So...how are you doing?" The comment was snide, I admit, but sometimes you have to have a little fun.

The business plan was simple in nature. It showed what I wanted to do and what I wanted to accomplish. It listed a few marketing strategies I was going to put into place. I enumerated how I saw the whole thing happening and my goals. It was not complex. For all intents and purposes your business plan needs to be simple and easy.

I've succeeded at every business I started to some degree and have never followed a business plan. They are complex and too data oriented. They lack real world functionality. The plans almost never work as they were intended. When the business succeeds, chances are, it will look much different than the path you wrote. A business plan is not necessary.

Keep your focus on what you want to accomplish, make a checklist every day of the things you need to do in order to succeed today. Repeat every day until success looks like you imagined it.

Your business model will change. Your learning curve will reshape itself. You may find something or people along the way that help you. The only certainty is that things will change. Evolve as your business does. Don't try to adhere to something that made sense on paper a year or two ago. The world is ever evolving and ever changing; you must, too, if you want to succeed.

11

Marketing 101: Getting the Business

I have made millions offering home services in various businesses over the years on less than a shoe string budget.

Whether it was Lawn and Landscaping, Window Cleaning, Deck and Fence Maintenance and Repair, Concrete Repair or House Painting, when anyone asked me what I did for a living I would say, "I am in marketing." I never said I stained decks, or that I was a concrete repairman. I have never been what I did for a living. I was always sure that what I did was really marketing.

Picking the best service provider

Who is the best house painter in your town? If you don't know, the answer is simple: the painter with the most houses to paint.

Homeowners don't base their decision on which house painter to hire on craftsmanship. The worst managers that do shoddy work still get business. The homeowners choose their painter because the sales person who signed them up for the service made them more comfortable than the competition. That is who gets the business.

The actual painters working on the house for him couldn't get the business and need to rely on someone else to get it for them. Lions are fed well. I am teaching you to be the lion and earn the lion's share.

The best and most reputable house painter in your town uses hired labor to paint houses. So is the owner of the company, the business man, the best painter in town? He certainly is the one holding the contracts to paint the houses, while the painters are begging for the work at $12 an hour. Do homeowners actually know that the painters there to paint the house are hired labor? Do they know the guy who sold them the job is only managing the job? Believe it or not, 99% of the time, they don't think about it. While you may be starting a service related company, you are really opening a marketing business for other service providers. To be successful in business, you must be successful at marketing. The name of the game is getting job after job after job, stacking them up and managing them well. Getting one job here and one job there would be a stressful waste of time and effort. You would be better off staying at the J.O.B. As a marketing professional, you have the business. Professionals in the trades you offer will be begging for the work.

Trust me. Place the ad we discussed earlier on craigslist for experienced painters to paint a home for $12 an hour. You will have 75 painters within an hour, begging for the work. It doesn't take long to figure out that holding the contract for the work pays more than doing the work itself.

You get the work. Let those who know the trade complete the work.

The very workers I hired along the way to do my jobs—jobs that I didn't know how to do at the time-- came on board to paint a house *and* to teach me how to do it. At $12 an hour it's the cheapest education you can buy. And you get paid while learning! Sound too easy to be true? It's not.

I am not going to teach you how to apply stucco to a home, to mud jack or replace a driveway or paint a house. But I will show you how to become an expert in your chosen field with enough expertise to impress your clients and win their business. I will show you how to get a book of clients within 2 weeks of starting your business.

Magical Secrets

Want to be a pro at marketing? Google how to market your business and you will be told every marketing secret there is. You'll be told to blog, to network, to gather a huge following on Twitter, max out with friends on Facebook and even—for a price—to market your business on Google using Google Ad Words.

That's only a start. There are millions of opportunities advertising on others sites in other ways. Everything from banners to pop-ups to click on ads.

Here's another secret: you can spend all your time and waste your money essentially throwing baby worms out into the vast ocean of the web in hopes of getting a bite; the quickest route to failure as a business is excessive spending on useless marketing. The internet is huge and the number of people doing all those things to get 'found' online is infinite.

There is no secret to mastering marketing online. If there were, everyone would know it and everyone would be a multi-millionaire by now. The secret doesn't exist.

Here's a secret that is real. Most of the guru's of marketing and many of the business pros have failed at their own business. Most of their success has come from teaching others how to do it. I won't name names, but many authors of how to get rich quick books or the how to quit your job and retire early book have had less than mediocre success in their own careers. They are really good at selling books and selling the dream.

When I started this one, I promised myself that I would only share things that were battle tested; things I have actually done and have taught to others. The 'secrets' don't exist, but hard work, clever common sense and determination are the best kept secrets.

In your Face!

Success in your new business relies on one thing: you have to be visible. You have to be in the public eye. You have to be seen.

For much of the world, the goal is convenience. Faster, easier, with less hassle gives the impression that you are navigating through life better. With this concept in mind, if you want to get in front of customers, you have to literally put your name and your services under their noses. Heaven forbid that they have to seek you out.

In today's high lightning-paced, digitally-addicted world, advertising online seems smart, doesn't it? A homeowner or customer would surely do research there. They would contact you and…think again. That's a fantasy.

I have placed over 2 million fliers on doors in homes around my hometown. I have probably placed 300,000 political signs. The cost is high. The time spent is high. But this is not about some getting rich quick scheme. We are not talking about a career sitting on your ass and clicking buttons on the computer. Running an online business and doing nothing all day is a bigger challenge than those other guys will tell you and they've written *that* book already.

The hard work of delivering marketing to door steps and street corners took the guess work out of my marketing.

You have to put your company name directly in front of the customer to ensure your success. Want more customers? Deliver more advertising. Want a referral? Ask clients to place a sign in their yard so you can get their neighbors' business. This kind of drip campaigning has worked for Taco Bell, Burger King, McDonalds and many others. It will work for you. When a client thinks of your particular service or product, you want them to think of you. They will if they've seen your name constantly.

Marketing 101

The Name

We've already discussed the importance of the name you pick but it is a topic important enough to expand. Think marketing when picking the name. Go for catchy and clever. Do not attempt to label based on characteristics for something in an attempt to sell yourself on values and responsibility, like Accountable Mud Jacking, or Integrity Housecleaning. Customers are interested in getting the lowest price and getting what they need to have done, done. Values and responsibility in a name are instantly forgettable. So pick a name that will stick out and set you apart. Google any service and you will get at least a few 'American' companies. American Plumbing, American Painting. What does this have to do with your business? That you are doing business in the United States? What does that tell any prospective customer? Are you name- dropping, using a country that is trillions in debt? Is that somehow important to your business? It makes no sense.

Pick a name that is noticeable and marketable. How do you want to grow your business down the road? Do you want to add other services? If so, leave your options open. Use something like **your last name** Industries. I own Peterson Companies. I add services all the time. I add DBAs as I expand. My curiosity and opportunities in the market converge with my passion to create more outlets for income.

Website

Though needing a website to get business is a myth, it is true that starting off, a website will help with your credentials. Contrary to popular belief, you will not get business from your website for a very long time after you have opened it. But homeowners (potential clients that have already found you) want to know you have a website. It is one of their qualifying questions. "Do you have a website?" "Yes, I do," results in an "Oh, ok. Wonderful," response. It's as though you are legit because you have a website. Having a website as a new business gives you clout, makes you appear established and qualified.

For a nominal fee you can buy a domain name through www.hippodaddy.com and have them design a website for your needs, both for the short term and with growth in mind. Add $12 a month for hosting and your website shows what you do, your address and your phone number. That's all that is needed.

Google and Bing, the two dominate web search

engines don't allow business start ups to rank high on search results from a phrase or word. Search engines, such as Google, are very picky about what companies can be placed on the 1st page of the listings, based on a variety of things. Seasoning, age authority, website content, reviews and testimonials from others sites, social media, etc., all are factors in to determining your visibility on the web.

Starting off, you need a name that tells what you do. It helps if your name can be the website domain, as well. Try to choose something as close to what a customer might put in a search engine inquiry as possible. If your company name is Chicago Driveway Replacement and a homeowner searches for 'driveway replacement in Chicago', you are going to rank higher in the search engine, resulting in greater visibility. Keep all of this in mind while choosing your name and purchasing your domain name. Go for maximum gain. Don't spend a bunch of money on your website. It is not needed yet. Once you are open and established, you can think about search engine optimization and paying for Google or other internet marketing. For now, get your doors open and start doing grass roots campaigning and guerilla marketing.

Political Signs

Direct line of sight advertisement to homeowners will bring business in.

You can spend tens of thousands for search engine optimization to fight for the top spot on search engines. Or you can almost double that much on large Yellow Book ads. Unfortunately, those are now dinosaurs. (How long has it been since *you* opened the Yellow Pages?) Or you can bypass all of that and get right to the homeowner.

I am talking about political or 'bandit' signs. I have literally brought in millions of dollars with these signs. If you learn anything from this book, learn this: Those who have more signs win.

Your signs should simply state what you do and the phone number. Nothing else is needed.

You aren't trying to brand yourself with these signs. You are trying to get the message out. You are in their neighborhood offering this particular service. Here is an example:

Deck~Fence
Staining and Sealing
111-222-3333

Now that you have your signs designed by a graphic designer, let's think about colors.

The more noticeable the better. I use a yellow plastic with black lettering. This is very noticeable. Simple message. Simple design. The more readable the better.

Now. How many should you purchase? As a rule of thumb, I always want to place 200 signs a week minimum on busy street corners and at the entrances of neighborhoods. This may seem like a lot, but during busy seasons I place more like 500 a week. You need to place 200 to see a response initially. That will help you gauge how many you need to place every week.

Politicians expect 1 vote for every 10 signs they place. For 200 signs, I most likely will get 20 phone calls. Those 20 calls will probably bring 10 new clients.

The math helps you compare how much it will cost you to have the signs made, how much it will cost you in time to go out and place them vs. how much money you bring in, based on those signs.

If I place 200 signs, set 20 appointments for estimates and close 10 clients at an average job of $850 a piece, I will bring in $8,500 gross. My cost for 200 signs is roughly $600. My gross profit after paying for the signs is $7,900.

This is guerilla marketing. Over the years, I have placed thousands of signs throughout cities I work in. Homeowners driving down the streets see the 'offer of service' and the phone number. In this cell phone world they call immediately. It's just that simple. Convenience and line-of-sight is direct marketing at its best- and fulfills a need. The prospective customer who calls is going to be the homeowner who knows they have to get their house painted soon, their deck or fence cleaned and stained or the leaky windows fixed or cleaned. The return on your investment is huge. And the speed at which you recover your marketing costs is almost instantaneous.

Place your signs out of the right of way. In most cities, this is 10 feet beyond the sidewalks of major intersections. At a busy intersection, you want to place the sign at a 45 degree angle to oncoming traffic. Visibility is high and away from the city right of way. City ordinance will enforce their rules and issue tickets if you don't follow this rule.

You also want to place signs at every neighborhood entrance in your city. Make sure the sign is at a 45 degree angle by the stop sign coming out of the neighborhood and in the line-of-sight with the driver. Make it visible and they will call.

Your starting minimum should be 200 signs a week.

Sign Droppers Beware

There is a risk. Many cities have ordinances against these types of signs. You could get fined. Having said that, I have brought in roughly 3 million dollars over the years and I have been fined $1800.

As with everything in life, reward comes with risk. If you could buy a $3 million dollar winning lottery ticket for $1800, would you? I would. I have. It has worked for me.

Why does this type of marketing work?

People procrastinate and are lazy. They may see their driveway needs worked on every time they drive out in the morning and come home at night. They may sit and look at their house that needs painted and think, "I need to paint my house." Finally, when they see a sign that says drive way replacement or house painting, they will call. They don't have to think about it when they are in front of the computer with a little time to search for something. They don't have to remember to put it on their list of things to do. They see your sign as they drive out of their neighborhood and are prompted to call. The 2nd reason this works is because signs are no threat. They aren't surfing the web and faced with the task of calling a corporation, or a large company that will charge a lot for this service. They are calling a small guy, perhaps a neighbor, the guy who is putting simple signs that say "this will be affordable." It also says "I am in the neighborhood; just call me."

The 3rd reason this works is because everyone is trying to master the online game, the referral business, the business they get from Realtors, etc. The competition is still saying "I have to call someone to analyze and fix my SEO." You actually ordered 200 signs and got out at midnight when traffic was light, to place them all over the city. That is what separates the successful from the bankrupt. You are hungrier than the competition and using methods outside of the box.

If you keep putting 200 signs a week minimum, on corners, even when people are pulling them up and knocking them over, you will be the one going to homes to greet the owner with a smile and give the him or her an estimate. You will be the one who sells them on your service. And you will do it all year long if that is what it takes.

You will have the phones monitored to await those phone calls that will be flooding in. It's just this easy.

Dollars and Sense

200 signs dropped per week = 20 incoming calls (10% return)

40% close ratio = 8 sales a week

$850 average per sale = $6800 a week in gross revenue

$27,200 a month in revenue = $272,000 in annual revenue in 10 months.

This is very realistic and will happen for you if you place 200 to 500 signs a week. Watch the business come in. Increase the number of signs to get more calls. It's like a faucet, turn it on or turn it off. Anytime you want, you can create the phone calls.

The income may vary with each particular trade, but this is gives you an example. If you paint houses at $2,500-$4,500 per job, your figures (and costs) will be higher than if you are doing deck and fence refinishing and selling an average $850 per job. I based the numbers on a 10 month year as most parts of the country have climate limitations for parts of each year. I, for one, like to take off a few months and enjoy the lifestyle I have designed for myself.

Cold Calling

Cold calling is a must in marketing. You have to get your name out there.

Whether you are doing painting, general contracting on homes, or working on decks and fences, you need to contact every realtor in your city twice. Yes. Twice. Every single realtor in the city must be contacted twice.

Lead master (www.leadmaster.com), an automated platform, or something similar, will make dialing easy and manageable. With lead master and a VOIP computer phone you can import thousands of names and numbers and click a button to dial hundreds of them a day. It also has the feature to leave voicemails automatically so you can record a message once every day and if they don't answer, you can push a button and it will deliver your pre-recorded message while you move to the next number.

As you dial, make notes on the clients you do talk to. You can designate a client as hot, warm, not contacted, or cold. Any variation you wish will help you organize your data base.

The system also sends out emails automatically and gives you reports of if and when they open the emails. You can also set reminders to alert you when you need to call a potential client again. The system is designed to maximize your efficiency with clients.

A few hundred dials a day is important when you're starting out. Once you get real busy, it becomes hard to stay on top of marketing calls. You're on jobs and handling the issues that come with managing the work.

Roughly 30,000 realtors in my area have been called. They all know about my business. It seems like a lot, but it isn't impossible.

This is also something you can outsource.

Mail Marketing

With today's technology driven marketing, email is now the mail box that is full of junk, rather than your home mail box. . Mail campaign return on investment (ROI) has grown over the last 10 years. With mail marketing, you can expect a 1%-2% return from contacts with a 30-40% close ratio on the clients who call.

If you send 10,000 pieces of mail and receive a 2% return, 200 potential clients are going to be interested in receiving a quote.

With 200 calls and an average close ratio of 35% you will perform 70 jobs from one blast of marketing. If your average profit is $1000 per job, the gross income from your mail blast will be $70,000 in revenue.

The letter you send must be cleverly written. You must give them a reason to call. A 10% discount or $200 off if they call by a certain date is often good incentive.

The envelope should be a #10 window envelope—the kind that has a clear portion where the address on the letter shows through--with a red stamp that says open immediately on it.

You can do a mailing in-house for as little as .28 a piece. You can outsource a bulk mailing for about 60 cents apiece.

The rate of return on your investment is the upside of mail marketing; the downside is the cost. Though bulk mail is less than first class postage, the cost is high due to the volume you need to send. In 2005, I was spending $100,000 a month doing mail marketing but had a return of $350,000 for my expense. The return made sense.

For mail marketing to make sense for you, you have a response rate of at least 1% and close 30% of those contacts to justify the expense. Once you get going, do it at least once to see if it is a viable option for you. Try getting that same return on web marketing. **It won't happen.**

Social Media

I personally do not do social media as a marketing technique. But without a doubt, you can make money by doing so. Using Face Book or social media such as Twitter or LinkedIn is the name of the game if you have many contacts to market to.

Social media is a valuable resource for finding people to market to, though. If realtors or other contractors are using it to market themselves, it may be a way of networking and connecting with them.

I have never once used social media to earn business. You can't be all things to all people and I offer enough trades and services that marketing them separately and effectively would be too time consuming for the response I could expect. I don't believe you have to use it and as everyone else has jumped on the bandwagon to get business, what I am showing you are untraditional ways to market your services to get you going quickly.

Flyers and Handouts

Flyers and other hand outs are good if used effectively. Generally, if you outsource this service, you'll be buried with 20 or more other companies trying to get attention that way. The trick is to do your flyer and handout marketing in house. It will cost less and make your business the only focus.

Contact a local high school or middle school and ask the front office how to place an ad for teenagers who want to make a little money placing flyers on doors in the neighborhoods around their school in the evenings or on weekends. You will usually have to go in and fill out paperwork, then they will post the ad in the office for students looking for a part time job. The labor can be as cheap as $9 an hour and you can hire as many as you can afford to place 300 flyers a night each in the neighborhoods you choose. In one night, with 3 kids working, you'll have 900 flyers distributed each night. At the end of the week that is 5000 flyers on very targeted markets as you would only choose neighborhoods that look like they need your service (house painting, mud jacking, deck and fence work, landscaping, cleaning, flooring, carpet, repairs and improvements, etc.) Whatever the service, place flyers only in areas where you think homeowners will buy from you.

The best case for distributing flyers is right after you complete a job in a neighborhood.

Put 'keeping up with the Joneses' letters on every door. A Joneses letter is designed to make the neighbors want to do what their neighbor did to their home. It lets them know that one of their neighbors trusted you and perhaps they should trust you as well. The following is an example:

We just put a new roof on your neighbor's house. We would love for you to take a look at it and ask the home owner how satisfied they are with our work. The address of the newly roofed home is

_____

Please ask your neighbor:

Are you happy with the job?

Was it affordable?

Are you happy with the service?

Did they fulfill your requests per the contract?

Was the yard clean and debris free when they left?

Do they offer a warranty?

We are confident they were pleased with the quality of our work. If your home also needs a new roof don't hesitate to call us at **123-456-7890.**

(Your company name)

Lowest price guaranteed

Highest quality guaranteed

20 years experience

Life time warranty

Insurance specialists

All major credit cards accepted

ABC Roofing
"Demonstrating integrity one shingle at a time"
123-456-7890

Although this example is for a roofing company, you can see how it could be used effectively. Yes, you can be bold and say you have 20 years of experience. The roofing crew you hire to fulfill the work may have a collective 40 years of experience. You can put about anything in your letter that you wish. Just be prepared to back it with the quality of your work.

Dirty Networking

Everyone needs to network. Everyone needs to associate with others in business in order to get business. Check with your local Chamber of Commerce to discover networking groups in your area. Find professionals looking to do the same. Networking forums can be useful if done correctly.

For networking to be effective, you have to give and provide opportunities to your fellow networkers. People complain about not getting business from their meetings but don't offer anything to other members. There is a reason that **WORK** is in the word, networking. It is work. You have to work for others in the group. Takers need not bother. Your group will fail you if you are "that guy" who shows up to a business meeting with a used car salesman attitude, searching for business. It is networking, not a sales pitch. Show up. Show as much interest in everyone else's business or career as you hope they will show yours. Find out what they do and see if you can help them or provide some service or refer a client who is looking for their service. You may find yourself earning business as well. The next time they have something that you might benefit from, you bet they will think of you. In networking, you have to work for others if you want others to work for you.

Spend Wisely

Marketing happens to be the largest industry on the planet. More dollars are spent on marketing, sales and advertising than any other thing in the business world. Many marketing companies attempt to sell marketing services to business owners, but if they know how to easily get the business and earn the client, why aren't they doing it themselves? Why are they still trying to find ways to market their services to you?

I have dabbled at spending money on other marketing services and without fail, every single time, I kick myself for it. For each client a marketing service brings in, that lead is sent out up to 10 times to service providers doing the exact same thing I am. It often generates the price wars that cause you to bid a lower price among the lions trying to feed on this one client. Do yourself a favor, do all of your marketing in house. Cut out all middle men. Stay lean and mean and save your money for higher return lower output marketing.

12

Sales 101

When you have a customer in front of you, you are not unusual if you are thinking, "How can I say the right thing in order to get this person to buy from me." That is exactly where your mind should be. However, in a service based business, the sale starts the moment the client calls. The call should be answered professionally. "Hi this is _____ (your company name or the name of the person answering the phone) How can I help you?" The customer hears "established" and "professional."

You should be ready with your calendar and pen in hand to take down information to set an appointment for an estimate and to end with an earnest thank you to the client for calling.

The second part of the sale occurs when you arrive at the home or location for the work. The most important thing about your presence is how you act. You must act, feel and believe on a deep level that this person wants to buy from you. He wants you to do the work. You must know on arrival he is about to sign the agreement you are going to write up as soon as you see what needs to be done. Act as if the contract will be signed. Act as if the work will be done. Act as if this person is your client. Somehow, some way, this one bit of advice, given to me a long time ago, has been the most important piece of information I was ever given about making sales. It is the law of attraction at work. It works every time.

If I go into a sale worried or fearful about whether the client will buy my services, the fear manifests and becomes reality. I will lose the sale. You must have the sale already signed, sealed and delivered in your mind. You will get the business every time; this should be your mindset.

When you arrive, don't park in the driveway. Park on the street. It's a gesture that says you are polite and considerate. If you are meeting the husband and the wife is about to leave for the grocery store, you having to re-park your vehicle before you can do a bit of business is embarrassing and a waste of time.

As soon as you see the client, smile. Make sure your smile is the first thing he or she sees. When you're in touching distance, extend your hand to shake, and look the soon-to-be client in the eyes. Thank him for inviting you over to do an estimate.

You may be self employed, but you do work for the client. They are essentially your boss.

After the hand shake, have a business card handy to offer them. In a matter of minutes (perhaps even seconds) you have smiled, shook their hand and looked them directly in the eyes, said a sincere thank you and handed them a business card. If you do this, you are ahead of 90% of your competition.

And remember, it's not always about the price. Many clients have chosen me over the competition even though my bid was up to 30% higher. It's about the sale, you and your company, not the price tag.

Your Presentation: 3 Things Set You Apart

Pick out at least 3 things about your process or service that you do better than the competition. It's all about presentation.

When the client shows you what he or she wants done, pay close attention. Let them talk. Be agreeable. If the client wants something that is not do-able or if their understanding of the problem is incorrect, don't interrupt them. Let them speak, explain what they want and feel heard.

If you are listening closely as they talk, they may say things that you can use later while delivering your sales pitch.

I once had a client who talked about his wife's garden and all of her plants. He was obviously proud of the Better Homes and Garden Backyard of the Year award they'd won and they enjoyed time spent in the yard. The yard and vegetation was important to these folks. The sale was no longer about a price tag. Now that he has shared this; the sale was about talking to him about his garden. Why would he tell a stranger so much information about his yard? He wants someone to care enough to listen to him. Now I talk to him about his plants and flowers and bushes. I talk to him about his garden and what he plants and ask questions about when to plant and how and at what times of the year. After 20 minutes of sitting in the sun talking about his yard and garden, he asks me inside to have a glass of iced tea.

Once inside, his wife offers me strawberries and he grabs the Better Homes and Garden magazine that features his yard.

Though I could care less about a yard, his home and yard are where I will make my money. I am a contractor and I offer services he needs. Each home and yard is worth about $1000.00 a year for me as I see it. And if he wants to talk about his favorite subject, for now, it is my favorite subject, too. By the time we get to the subject of the deck needing power washed and refinished, I am ready to deliver with a great sales pitch and a good price tag.

What the client doesn't know is:

#1. The time spent sharing his hobby with me has made him more comfortable with me. I have done nothing but listen. His degree of comfort is greater, all on his own doing.

#2. The price has gone up.

Why? Because I know all I need to know to present this for a little higher price for very special (but normal) service.

The first thing I will mention when I start my sales pitch is that the guy who stained his deck the last time didn't do him any favors. I will tell him, "I do things a little differently than the competition. I won't just power wash this deck and slap some stain on it. If I do, you will be calling me in a few years and it won't be to ask me how nice my day is."

I have earned his trust by now so I can delicately tell him that the last guy didn't do a great job. I can present him with a lengthy explanation of applying deck wash and an oil based stain. Commercial Grade? I guess so. I buy it from a commercial paint store. Acid wash? The bottle from Home Depot that says the deck cleaner is acid. But now, I am presenting a product, a service with expertise behind it. I am no longer just the guy saving him the back pain of doing it himself. I am offering a finished product and service that he himself can't do as well as I can.

The next thing I'm going to tell him is that the acid wash we use is eco friendly. It is non toxic to his plants and flowers. This is obviously something important to him.

I will then tell him about my experience. It will be like the resume everyone puts together. I'll inflate it a little and make it sound good. This is a job interview, remember? I must sound and look professional and like I know, better than most, what should be done. I would say something like, "I have done over 2000 decks like this and honestly, I'd like to see this deck on my website because your yard is so pretty. This guy is now in love with me. Better homes and Gardens and a company to showcase his yard online? He is thrilled. And if I am going to put his deck on my website, I better make it look good. He feels good.

Now I will give him my spiel about how we carefully prep the wood using a 4200 PSI power washer. Besides sounding real cool, I am making it sound important. Does that mean someone with a 3200 psi power washer can't do the same job as I can? The truth is a guy with a 2800 PSI power washer can. But I sound like I have invested in the most powerful equipment on the market and this makes the difference.

I talk about soaking the deck and sometimes scrubbing with the acid wash to opens the pores on the wood to allow better penetration. While this is true, it is also sales grease. I'm buttering up the process!

You must do this to win business. I have sold him on my business, inflating the process. My experience and sounding like a true professional make him sure that his garden and flowers will be well cared for, and I am going to put the job on the website as a showcase job.

Now, I am taking shots of the deck with my camera phone, telling him I need 'before' photos.

I still haven't presented a price tag.

You must find angles to discuss with each and every client. I can't begin to tell you what scenario you should use or how to find commonality with each specific person. I can tell you the price tag is less important than the person feeling comfortable with you. You must find something to talk about. You'll gain credit for caring, not just about the sale, but you also care about this client's life.

Present the price

With your carbonless copies in hand and a calculator, you are now going to figure out the price for your services.

We will talk in more detail about pricing, profit, and costs later. But when you are pricing out your services, you have to be cautious of a few things. The first thing to remember is no one wants you to get rich. And no one wants to pay more than they need to for a service. Especially not this client. So you must break your costs down and bury your profit. Here is how using a deck staining job as an example:

Prep Chemicals $85
Power Washing and Prepping $275
Sundry Supplies $45
Stain $340
Labor $350

The above price tag is $1,095. I have broken it down into the various costs. This approach is the best and your carbonless copies should reflect such line items for costs.

The first charge of $85 is for prep chemicals. They will probably cost about $15 at Home Depot. But the homeowner does not need to know that the "acid" you use is that inexpensive. Most dealers or service providers have a percentage markup of their supplies. This is hidden profit.

The power washing and prep cost will most likely cost you $40 for $10 an hour per worker to power wash his deck for 4 hours. He is not surprised at this cost after the big deal you have made of how you prep the decks with a 4200 PSI and take your time to acid wash and scrub it to make sure all the pores of the wood are open. (Nothing about this is a lie; it's what the acid wash does. You have just expanded it a bit). So $275 looks justified once you've told him how hard you are going to work on it.

The next item is sundry supplies. This will cover plastic, tarps, job specific things as tape and rags, etc. Your truck or that of your contract workers will have plenty of this on it. The $45 will just pay for anything you use or need.

Now the stain is a high grade commercial grade sealant. Though no one makes a low grade homeowner developed grade sealant, it sounds real good. The stain you'll use is roughly $28 a gallon at contractor pricing. You are not offering the customer contractor pricing. You are selling the stain for what the homeowner would buy it for. In this case, it would be about $45 a gallon. When you tell him 8 gallons at

$45 a gallon, you are showing him the actual cost of the stain to him. He has no idea you are making money on the stain, too.

Now, when you get down to labor, you will say, "And I will charge you $350 for me and my crew to stain your deck." The labor seems reasonable, he doesn't think I am getting rich and I have presented the price by breaking it down item by item.

And just like every infomercial you've ever seen, it's time to throw in the "If you call right now we will throw in another set for free" line. Only in this case, it is not an infomercial and I say, "Say yes now, today and I will offer you a $100 discount. I'd love to put your home on my website and have you for a referral."

Keep in mind that before I even priced the deck, I already added $100 in there. I should only be charging about $800 for this deck but he talked my ear off and I felt he was comfortable with me. I sold him on everything he wanted and offered him a special discount of $100. How can he say no?

He signed the agreement and I collected a deposit. Sometimes homeowners frown upon a deposit being required, but get the deposit. Always protect yourself from not being paid. Once the homeowner pays the deposit, they are hooked in. They can't randomly decide to use another service provider without telling you. Countless times, I have not taken a deposit and the client decided to use another service provider who is cheaper, sometimes after I had bought materials for the job, not to mention the hours spent talking to them about each step, and the how, when and why. After I drove off, they decided "I will use the other guy. He's cheaper." Once they pay me a deposit, they are officially a client.

In other cases, clients didn't want to pay in a timely manner after the job was done. Without the deposit, I would have been out of pocket for the expenses for labor and the materials the job took to complete. Take your deposit. It is for your protection. Don't worry about clients not liking it. Good clients will pay the deposit with few questions; bad clients will not want to pay. It will all work out in the end.

I shook his hand and told him I was glad to meet him and that I would be in touch.

Discover the Professional within You

I just gave you an example of a deck estimate and how I would approach the sale. That type of sales pitch works in any industry.

If I am presenting Mud Jacking I tell a potential client, "I don't pump mud like the competition." This is very true. My company, www.Bossmudjacking.com, does not pump mud under slabs. It's even bold and very visible on my agreement. (Never use the word contract, it represents bad meanings for many people and scares them. We are in a Politically Correct world where things must sound nice. Contracts vs. Agreements are one of those things.)

We use a mixture of Sodium Bentonite, Portland Cement and Sand. This mixture holds up far better than soil and doesn't retract or shrink after drying out. The top soil mix that most of my competitors use is cheaper and can lower the price tag, but I can charge more because I'm selling a much better product. I talk about Sodium Bentonite when I'm giving a sales pitch. I talk about all of its uses, the expense of the material, how my process is much better than the competition. "You can get cheaper," I will say, "but you will get what you pay for." I don't try to be the cheapest in town; I try to be the professional, the one who offers a better product and service. Even when the economy is bad, the majority of people want quality and are willing to pay for it.

If I go to a Mud Jacking bid and determine that I can't repair with Mud Jacking and the slab must be replaced, I am not going to give the buyer the cheapest bid so they will use me. I will go into great details, first asking questions such as, "How long do you plan on staying in this house?" I ask this to know whether a low bid is warranted. If he is interested in selling soon, quality may not be his hot button.

If the answer is, "We plan on staying here forever," I begin by saying something like, "Generally, a builder's grade driveway can be torn out and replaced for about $6 a square foot. However, if you want good quality concrete that you won't have to worry about doing this to you again,"--as we study his cracked and broken concrete--"You will be more in the $8-$9 a square foot range." I am opening it up for a higher quality sale with a higher price tag. I give him both options; he will decide what he wants.

If he goes with the low price I make money. If he goes with the higher price, I make even more money. Win, win.

I tell him more about the expensive concrete mixes available and explain that all concrete isn't created equal. It's not.

I will make factual statements or ask rhetorical questions. "A higher quality mix that uses granite in the mix is much harder and will last forever." "Can you imagine commercial buildings built on builder grade concrete?"

You want to get their mind agreeing with that fact that all concrete is not created equal. Who is going to be pouring the new drive for this client? Concrete workers who don't know how to earn the business like you now do.

You will simply go to concrete finishers and offer them the job. You are a marketer remember? These sales tactics work and work very well. You are the professional, experienced and conscious service provider. You are giving the customer options. Everybody loves to order from a menu. Give them options. Just make sure to have your profit built into any option you present.

If I was selling a house painting job, I would tell the client, "It's all about the prep." And it most certainly is. I would boldly say I have the best prep in town. Did Henry Ford build his automotive empire by telling investors and the government that he didn't have the best product available? Once he had competition, who was to say if his automobiles were better? 'Better' is subject to interpretation. But remember, people need to hear what they need to hear, most of the time. Most want you to tell them they are buying the best they can buy. If they knew what was best for them, they wouldn't have asked for an estimate and your opinion to begin with. They would have just contracted for the best and been done with it.

I will tell a customer the difference between a good paint job and a bad one is the prep and the quality of the caulk. This is absolutely true. Most contractors use cheap caulk, yet use 30 year or life time durability paint. Using caulk that will hold up no more than 2 years and paint that will hold up for 30 years makes zero sense. Not only that, you aren't offering a valuable and professional service. I will tell the client, "I use caulk designed for maximum temperature fluctuations for the Midwest heat and cold." It sounds fancy but all I'm saying is that I use premium caulk. I will delicately tell them that they don't want to go with someone who doesn't use high end caulk and high end paint or take the time to prep correctly. If the painter they hire doesn't spray enough paint on, the client will be paying to do this again in just a few short years.

This is fear based selling. It is putting doubt in the client's mind about going 'cheap'. Clients want to know that what they are buying will last a long time. You are no different, right? Make sure your product will last a long time. Delicately put fear in them about the competition and get them to rethink using someone cheaper instead of you, based on the expertise, your knowledge and the precautions you will take. You will win the sale, even with a higher price tag. You will win the battle if they believe that you care enough to teach them about the process, what not to do and how you are going to do it right. Being a professional means that you don't have to be price driven. If anyone with a paint brush can paint a house and those who are now marketing themselves as painters only differentiate their service by price, you win by knowing the angles.

Never be the sales person going to a home and hoping to make the sale because you are the cheapest provider of any service. Being the low cost provider will inevitably take you right out of business.

From Blue to White Applied: Selling points

If you want to hang the work shirt up and put on the boss's attire, go out and be the Boss, you now have the responsibility to sell what your workers do.

So what about your choice of business? What angles and specifics about your trade do you need to emphasize in order to get the business?

What shortcuts do providers take in your trade?

What can you promise the client that you will do better than the competition?

What are hot button issues for clients?

What fear can you utilize to make a client weigh using you vs. the low cost provider whose only selling point is 'CHEAP'?

What benefit will the customer see long term by using you?

I can't begin to teach you every angle of every trade, but following is a brief list of examples you can use and build on. You'll learn more along the way.

Don't use all of these. You'll want to pick and choose at least 3 things that you will do differently than your competition.

And remember, I am not telling you to promise without delivering. You must have integrity. If you say you will do these things and use these claims to make the sale, you must follow through. The added value and integrity allows you to charge more because you are truly better. These are techniques to build the reputation of being a good service provider.

House Painting

We use premium 30-year paint.

We only use the highest quality caulk that will last in the hot and cold climate.

My painters don't prep the house. You see, painters are paid when the house is painted, so the faster they paint the house, the faster they get paid. I use a separate crew to prep the house to ensure the highest quality prep job. Then I focus on my painters being the highest quality painters. Two separate processes ensure high quality on both jobs by preventing cutting corners on either aspect of the process.

Before we paint, we power wash the house and use cleaners to ensure a clean surface for the paint for maximum adhesion.

I will mask the areas that are not to be painted. I will make sure paint does not touch concrete, cars, or anything else that you don't want painted.

I will make sure the house has a 3 MM coat when we are finished. Often times, the competition does not apply enough, and the job shows shadows and light spots as it ages.

I caulk every crack, nail hole, seam, imperfection, and susceptible area to prevent wood rot from occurring due to moisture.

Most companies spray the paint on. I do spray, but most of the time we back roll and brush it like it used to be done.

High quality is what we are about; house painting is expensive. You don't want to have to paint again in 5 years.

I let them know that I am not the cheapest in town. I let them know that cheap is just that... CHEAP. I may be only a few hundred dollars higher than the competition, but what if they have to repaint this soon because the low price guy did it cheaply? Give them an emotional insurance policy that they have made the right decision.

Concrete Finishing/Pouring

Not all concrete is created equal.

The concrete you need to replace is 'builder grade' concrete. You can replace it for $5-6 a square foot, but it will be the same quality as this. I suggest a harder mix, a mix that will last. The additional amount you pay to get the higher quality mix is your insurance policy that it won't crack like this again.

Again, concrete is not created equal. Can you imagine a high rise building built on the mix this builder used?

I like to place plenty of rebar in the concrete. I space it every 10 inches to maximize the strength of the concrete.

For $8 a square foot I can pour a driveway that you will never have to replace again.

Once the driveway has dried and cured, I come back

and apply a commercial grade sealant to protect it from moisture, the elements, salt, etc. That is included in my price.

Deck and Fence Staining

We don't offer a labor only service; we offer a product that will save you money long term.

We aren't just here to do the hard work of applying stain to the deck. You could do that yourself over a weekend. We use a special process to prep the deck for maximum adhesion of the new stain.

The products and stain we use are commercial grade. You cannot find them in a hardware store.

If you are staining this deck every 2 years, you will get 4 years from my process and materials, saving you money in the long term.

The competition will power wash the deck and apply stain. This makes little sense. The stain is designed to repel water. Water at high pressure doesn't change that. We apply chemicals to open the wood pores; we apply chemicals to remove the adhesive qualities of the stain so we can apply the new stain to the wood. Have you ever heard of Mill-Glaze? Mill Glaze or Mill Wax is an industrial lubricant that is applied when your wood is cut in order to create a clean cut on your wood and prevent burn marks on the wood. It preserves the mill's blades and acts as a wood preservative while it sits on a train, on a truck, or in a lumber yard. You can't see the wax on there, but it is on there, if the contractor didn't remove it before he stained it. It is like staining wax paper. The stain never hit the wood to penetrate deeply. That is why you have to stain it so often. I will fix that issue, using mill glaze remover so the stain will last you longer.

I protect your landscaping and home. I mask everything off so no stain will get anywhere other than where it needs to be.

Mud Jacking

We offer a long term solution to erosion and falling concrete, rather than your typical mud jacking solution. We use a non- organic material, designed to prevent erosion.

Rather than using top soil, water and a bit of mortar for our mix, we use sodium bentonite, mason sand, and Portland cement.

Instead of using an organic material, we use a high yield, high PSI material that withstands water and drought so you don't have to continually fix this issue.

Unlike the competition, we don't simply pump a thick mix to act as a pier under the drive and then lift it back up. We fill the entire void and then bring the slab up. If all voids are filled so you don't have to worry about it sinking again.

House Cleaning

We use all English speaking help.

We are insured.

Not only are we insured, but we formally introduce you to our cleaners and use the same ones every time so they can learn your likes and preferences.

We offer basic weekly or bi weekly cleaning or we can do a thorough deep clean that will make your home as sanitary as a hospital.

We want to make cleaning easy on you. Once you try us a few times and we get to know how you like things done, we want you to feel comfortable with us cleaning whether you are there or not.

For every two week service for one year, we clean one week free. We'll clean once or twice to make sure we're meeting your needs and then the third week will be on us if you agree to have us clean for you for one year.

We leave you a special check list that you fill out to

tell the maids exactly what needs to be done every time to make sure you are getting what you want.

Marketing Buttons

All of these things are true, but it is also marketing. These are 'hot buttons' for specific services. You must deliver what you promise and follow through. These sales pitches and closing assertions will get the sale done. If not, you have educated the customer and he or she will remember those details when making the decision at a later date. These marketing hot buttons will win sales for you.

Resources are Available

Visit our website for plenty of resources, including more sales pitch points for additional trades. We're available to coach you and help you every step of the way. The trade you choose is not as important as the methods you will use to reach your goals. Together, we can help you find the service you want to provide and assist you to ensure your success.

13

10 Sales Rules to Follow

Rule #1: You have to be sold first.

You are the service provider/business owner. You need to be out there selling and marketing your business until you evolve to the point you have other sales help. For now, it's only you.

So you are the one meeting customers and responsible for making the sales. But you must be sold on your services before anyone else will be. You have to believe your services are valuable, your time is valued and the final product you deliver will be top notch. There will be nothing out there that is better. *You* have to know you are better than the competition in some fashion.

You have to be convinced you deserve success. You can't go out and be happy-go-lucky, hoping to put on a good performance if you yourself aren't sold on the fact that you deserve success.

Before you can sell yourself to that client, before that client can be convinced to choose you over the competition that you are the person for the job; you have to be entirely certain that you are sold on YOU, INC. Once you know that, everything begins to fall in place; everyone else will be convinced you are the person to hire, too. A business owner without conviction is soon a failed business owner looking for a J.O.B.

Rule #2: People want to buy; they don't want to be sold.

Sales often take a bad rap. No one enjoys dealing with a pressure sales guy.

When I first got into sales, I had negative conceptions about sales and sales people. I didn't ever want to be the guy trying to push someone into buying something. I didn't want to act happy and on top of the world while I dealt with a client and then come back down to reality after the sale, back to my real personality. I especially didn't want to be someone I'm not, just to get someone else to like me and to buy from me. The good news? I found out I didn't have to do any of those things. Neither do you.

To be a good sales person, you have to be direct and clear in your message. You have to be concise. You have to quickly tell a potential client what they need to hear about your service and about any additional benefits they will get by using you. You have to tell them why they should want to use you. Fear-based selling is something I regularly use to get my clients. I delicately tell them of what they don't want to do or what they don't want to have happen. I provide them with reasons to think I am the expert. Being an expert means that I need to know 90% more than 10% of the population does. By now, you know more about being self employed than 10% of the population. You are now an expert at being self employed. It truly is just that simple. Now go back to Sales Rule #1: do you believe it? You must if you want to win.

Allow people to buy from you; allow people to make their own decisions. Pressure is good when it allows tires to be aired up and basketballs to bounce. But too much pressure can explode either a basketball or a tire. You'll have a break down or have to end the game. Keep your pressure low. Inform and educate the client. Be professional. Allow them to buy from you. In short, don't be a salesman, be a professional.

Rule #3: It's all about presentation.

The cards you hold, the agreements the clients sign, your attire and how you present yourself is all very important. You again look the part and put on a good, professional presentation.

Your sales approach must be refined and refined. Practice your presentation and your delivery, time after time. Practice with a friend; try it a few times before you go into battle. Make sure you have your business cards. Make sure you go through the steps that will ensure that your work is complete. Be sure to deliver on your promises so that *you* know why you should be the chosen for the job. Make sure you do what you do better than the other guys who are trying the same thing. Then you can be a better presenter than the next guy. It's a must.

Rule #4: Passion is contagious, but not as contagious as enthusiasm.

It's Monday and 98 degrees outside. You've been sweating all day, out there signing up clients and collecting deposits for your services. The calls are coming in from the signs you've placed, the phone calls you made to realtors and others are coming in. You've joined a few networking groups and business is booming. You are about to go meet a client to make the 8th estimate and sales presentation of the day and you are tired. Worn out. You feel you are saying the same things again and again and all you want to do is go home. This scenario **will** happen.

You have to meet that 8th client of that hot and sweaty day with as much enthusiasm as you did the 1st sale you ever made. You have to have as much passion and enthusiasm in the PM as you had in the AM. The passion and confidence radiating from you will touch everyone you talk to; it will increase your chance of making the sale. Be confident; be passionate about what you do and what you provide. You will succeed.

Admittedly, your duties can get monotonous, but look at stand-up comedians, rock and roll bands and public speakers. They travel the world, saying (or singing) the same things over and over again. They have to say or sing the same things for the 5000th time with as much enthusiasm this time as the very first time. You have to adopt this mentality and make it your rule. Determine to be the same way you were the 1st time you made that 1st big sale.

Rule #5: Stories sell, people tell.

Telling the customer what they need to hear only goes so far. You have to tell them a story. People love stories. Stories take them out of the current moment and get them engaged in something other than the decision they may need to make today.

Often, I will look at the project I'm estimating and say, "I did one of these a few weeks ago not to far from here." I describe the similarities and tell the customer what the other client wanted. I offered X choices to make the finished product last longer and to save money in the long run.

Stories of other clients using your service are always powerful. Testimonials sell. A good story to back up your experience or to humor the client is even better. Humor goes a long way when dealing with people. Any chance you get, use laughter to lighten things up.

Rule #6: You are a consumer too; act like one.

Sales people often forget that they are consumers, too. They consequently forget that customers are spending their hard earned money. Most clients won't have an abundance of that. They are working hard, just like you, to survive and hopefully thrive. Always be mindful of what people will and won't spend and make your presentation accordingly.

If you are cavalier in your approach to spending $1800 on something and act like it is such a bargain, it's a steal, they will be turned off. It's much better to say "I know $1800 can be a kick in the pants, but this will prevent further problems that may save you 4 times that later."

It's the attitude, not the circumstance that makes the difference. Always strive to understand the consumer's situation and respect their money the same way you respect yours. If you are a respectful seller, your buyers will respect you.

Rule #7: Don't be a know it all.

When under the pressure to make a sale, it is easy to act and play like you know all to ins and outs of everything.

Customers pick up on that attitude, even if you don't think they do or mean to exhibit it. It is always best to give them an honest, "I don't know," rather than to come up with an answer that may or may not be right. Assure them that you will ask someone you trust and get back to them with an answer to their question. Being a professional at what you do is necessary; knowing everything isn't. Let your potential clients see the human side of you. Admitting you don't have knowledge about something they ask gives you the chance to also show that you are dedicated enough to find out anything you need to know.

Rule #8: Listen twice as much as you talk.

There is a reason you have 2 ears and one mouth. You were designed to listen.

Listening to your client is a must and will give them comfort that you really want to hear what they have to say. I can't tell you how many times I have sat through long explanations of what someone wanted when I already looked at the job and knew exactly what I was going to do regardless of their story. It's a must. Listening will also help you find the customer's deeper, hot buttons or buying triggers issues.

Clients want to be heard. You want to make the sale. Listen intently, talk less than you listen, and use what they tell you to prepare your sales approach.

Throughout the meeting, the client wants to know that you know what she or he wants. You can give them that assurance by simply listening, then showing them that you listened by using what they told you to make the sale. You have successfully done what most sales people don't: listen.

Rule #9: Rushing is a no-no.

Most clients hire me days after the sales meeting. If I push too hard for the sale the first time I meet them, it goes poorly. It is a great chance to lose the sale. You have to be patient, listen and then let the client decide on their own terms.

Don't rush. Do make sure you do a thorough presentation. Completely inform the client without rushing them in any manner. They are deciding whether to spend money with you. If you rush them; they won't. A sale takes time, time to build trust, time to establish rapport. Allow the time to make this happen.

Rule #10: Sell benefits, not price.

Sales people who sell price over benefits rarely sell anything.

Believe it or not, price is the smallest concern in a sale. Price always matters and people always want to know the price. But what they are spending on is a service. I have sold jobs for much more than my competition because I sold the benefits of my service. I sold the bells and whistles. I sold tangible products and results rather than savings. I got the job.

I almost never offer the lowest price in the market. And I will tell people upfront, "I am not the cheapest in town, but I do it right. You can have faith in my work." I may market myself as the "lowest price guaranteed", but by the time I present my price tag to them for any service, it won't be the cheapest. Rather, it will be the cheapest for the high quality I provide. The benefits are what matters.

Sell what they are getting for your price.

14

Profit and Pricing

Considering how to price anything can be a daunting task. How do you price something to sell in today's market, and yet make enough money to live the lifestyle that you want to live?

It can be hard to do. If you follow a few simple rules, you will not be 'giving away the farm' unintentionally. Often, people are so eager to earn the business, they forgo the rules and consequently give such low bids that it doesn't cover the costs associated with doing the work. Or more often the case, they offer a good price and then offer way more services for the price tag agreed upon. Either way it will bankrupt a company if too much of this is done.

On the other hand, some companies are so intent on certain pricing, they price themselves out of the market.

As a new business owner, it is important to find that middle ground.

First things first: determine what you want to make a year. This is the most crucial part of the formula. It doesn't matter what service you will sell in the marketplace just yet. It matters what you need to make. Let's start there.

Let's say you need to make $120,000 a year to pay your bills and live comfortably. You have ten months to bring this money in before the weather will be a problem. (Or before your extended vacation—whichever.)

120,000 divided by 10 months a year equals 12,000 a month you need in income.

This should be the first part of your plan, knowing what you want to make this year.

The #1 rule I always follow for pricing my services is to never make less than 35% after all expenses are paid.

As a general contractor, I have people calling me for various things daily. Many people ask if I paint houses or build decks or repair wood rot or replace windows or build fences or do Mud Jacking or any other variety of things. My answer is always, "Yes, I do."

Because it is not me who actually does these things, I can say yes to anything. I am in what industry? If you said marketing, you are right. People in the above mentioned trades will be doing the work. I just need to bring the work in for them.

So, I never do anything for less than 35%.

Let's say it is a house painting job and I sell the job for $4200. By the time I pay a crew to prep the house, buy the materials, pay the crew to paint the house and cover whatever marketing I have done to bring that call in, I must net $1,470. $1,470 is 35% of the gross sale and I plan to put that in my pocket.

If I am offering the service directly through one of my full time in house crews, such as deck and fence staining, or Mud Jacking, or roofing, I will make closer to 70% profit.

Never compromise your company by giving things away too cheap. It is easy to "only charge" $500 because you don't feel that you are working all that hard for the money and you'd really like 'this' job, but being self employed means you have many more expenses than are reflected in each job. Always honor your company and your own hard work by standing by your expectation of a reasonable profit for your company. After all, you are the owner of it and the care taker of it.

In-house vs. Brokering services

When considering whether to do things 'in-house' or to hire jobs out to independent contractors, it comes to one question: How profitable do you want to be?

Many factors must be considered when answering that question.

How to G.C.(General Contract) any Service

The first factor you must consider is your time. How much time are you willing to spend to make money performing a specific trade?

Let's say that you decide to offer house painting as your service. If someone asks you to build a deck, will your standard answer be the same as mine? Will you say, "Yes, I do."

What you are really saying when you say "Yes, I do," is that you will find someone who knows how to do that. You'll be the middle man (or broker of services) you'll find someone to help you with pricing the detailed information about doing the work.

Here's where the 'how much time' question comes in. How much time do you want to spend on that deck building job? Your margin needs to be no less than 35% and closer to 75% depending on your time.

The higher visibility companies are going to be charging more for services than Joe 6-pack who is out of work and needing a job to pay the light bill. The higher priced company has marketing to pay for—which is what made them more visible--trucks and vans, fuel bills, office space, cell phones, company paid employee insurance, etc. Joe 6 pack, who is just as skilled at building a deck as the higher priced company only has to pay for his house, his light bill, food. His overhead is much smaller and so is his profit margin.

If you outsource or broker your sale to the higher priced company, that company will most likely provide great service, be insured, and won't expect payment until the service is done correctly. You won't have to be on the jobsite babysitting in order to have the job done right. They already have people in place to babysit their employees. (And those bosses also need to get paid from your job).

If you hire Joe 6 pack, he knows exactly what the high priced company knows to get the job done right. The deciding factor is your time. How much does Joe need to be watched and monitored? How much do you need to be looking over his shoulder? How much babysitting can you afford to do? How profitable do you need to be?

Profit and Time

If you broker it out to the larger company, you will make your 35% or less, depending on how good you are at getting the expensive company to do it at a sub contractor price. If you hire Joe 6-pack, your 75% profit will make up for some of the jobs you may lose since you are not marketing and selling while you are monitoring. More time invested=more money; less time invested=less money. At the end of the day, your name is on the company and the job must been done well. Whoever you hire must do it well and it is up to you to decide how much time you'll devote to the job, which should determine the pricing. You must ensure quality.

A Pricing Scenario

Back to your $120,000 a year in income.

Let's say you've decided to offer house painting as your main service. Depending on your geographic location, you intend to sell the average home painting job for $3700. Here is a typical scenario. Expenses on that $3700 price tag:

$300 in signs or marketing dollars that brought in that client

$240 in labor for 1 crew of 2 men prepping the house for one full day at $12 an hour for a 10 hour day

$60 for 2 cases of high quality caulk

$650 in paint and supplies

$576 for 2 professional painters $18 an hour each for 16 hours your profit will be $1,874 on this house painting job.

If you use this formula and utilize the resources I've given you, you will need to paint 67 houses this year to clear $120,000. If you plan to work 10 months out of the year, you will need 7 houses a month to paint. Does that sound like a lot? It's not. I paint 10-20 houses a year and don't do a bit of marketing for it. If I did market the service, I would probably paint more than 150 houses a year. You can, too.

Let's say you decide you want to hire the higher priced, more visible company to do your work. Joe 6-pack just went to work for them and you don't want to start the babysitting process over again. You sold the job for $3700 and hand it over to the higher priced company to complete. You hire the company for $2800, leaving you little to worry about except collecting the money and giving away more profit. But with few headaches and no babysitting you have more time to find more jobs. In this case, you would make $900 and would have to paint 145 houses a year to make your $120,000 annual income. It all comes down to profitability and time spent on the job itself.

Another Scenario

I own Boss Mud Jacking, a national company that does Mud Jacking and Concrete Repair. I invested roughly $50,000 for my first truck, the equipment, trailers and tools to start the business.

After doing my market research and completing a few jobs, I discovered what we were capable of. I knew my crew could bring in $2800 completing 2 jobs a day with my equipment. This was my benchmark: 2 jobs a day. I planned on working 10 months a year, traveling abroad for 2 months and making $600,000 a year in Mud Jacking. My general contracting company is also operating.

In Mud Jacking, you literally are pumping dirt or cement like material under concrete. The materials are cheap and the profit is astounding. A typical job for $1,400 will cost $100 in materials, $100 in labor and a nominal amount for fuel for the equipment. Once I account for the 50 signs I placed to pull in a client, I will have made an astonishing $1130 on a $1400 job.

The return is enormous. The profit margin often exceeds 80% and I can do 2 jobs a day for 10 months a year working 23 days a month. Annual income: $600,000 in revenue.

Here is my business model, step by step:

> #1. Place 600 signs a week across the city, making my business a city-wide bill board.
> #2. Cover every phone call that comes in and make sure an appointment is set for an estimate.
> #3. Make effective presentations and bring in 3 jobs a day.
> #4. Complete 2 jobs a day, every day, 23 days a month.
> #5. Repeat. If I didn't do this in-house, I would have to refer the business to another company and I would earn only 20% or so.

This model would not work as well if I outsourced it. Some services work better than others with outsourcing. This one doesn't. Why would you leave 400K on the table? I didn't. You don't have to either. The trick to running a home service based business in-house is having trained staff ready and able to complete the work for roughly $12 an hour per employee. Make sure they are good at what they do. Efficiency is key. In order to do 2 jobs a day, 23 days a month, your employees need incentives.

For now, know that services provided in-house require steady management. The payoff is usually higher and you can handle a lot of volume if you follow my very simple model.

How to treat your help.

It is no secret that the primary reason most people become self employed is because they can't stand working for someone else. The long hours, the lack of respect, the few "thank yous" that are handed out; are not thanks enough for the back breaking work required.. The Just Over Broke compensation that barely pays the bills with little opportunity to make more is enough to wear anyone out. The physical stress wears down the body, the emotional stress tests the soul.

Give them what they want.

Once you find good help, treat them well. Good help *is* hard to find.

Though technically as contract laborers, they work for themselves, but they are working for you. Since you have the skills to find the jobs, they rely on you for their well being and peace of mind. You provide them with work, therefore you feed their family. In corporate America it seems a suit and a tie earns respect. But if you spent a day with my guys in the field, you would have more respect for them than any number of starched shirt number crunchers who sit behind a desk. In the blue collar world, people sweat daily. They pick up 150 lb bundles of materials, scale roofs, and climb 40 foot ladders with 80 lbs on their shoulders. These guys deserve respect and a thank you.

Too often, your check is your only thank you. Bosses or business owners who treat the help like they are doing them a favor will learn some hard lessons. Gratitude is powerful. If you aren't grateful for your hard working team who get up and come to work for you day after day, you will create a cancer in your company that will be difficult to remove. One bad attitude spreads to others and will rot your company from the inside out.

Pay a decent wage, but think about your help's lifestyle. Can you afford to buy them lunch a few times a week? If you can, then you should. After all, it is a tax write off. I would rather spend it on eating pizza and having a few beers with my guys after work to celebrate a job will done or maybe just make a bad day better than to send it to Uncle Sam.

Can you handle letting them think for themselves? Then you should. Aside from telling my crews where and when to be on a job, I trust them do the job on their own. I don't manage, nitpick them, or drone on and on. The good help I find I trust to do a good job.

That's one of the things that make them good help. For the most part, they are self-employed because they want to be free; they do not want to be controlled or managed. A man (or woman) wants to be able to make decisions on their own and to have a say in how things go. They want to be heard and respected.

Give them the respect they deserve.

Can you stomach your guys wanting to leave early for the day so they can go do something personal for their own 'lifestyle design'? Then you should. Work will be there, time lines and deadlines will, too. Pay your help well but provide a better lifestyle for them, too. In return you will get mentally sound, emotionally stable employees who are dedicated and loyal. They will be happier and work harder for you knowing that you want the same things for them as you want for yourself.

Technically, the guys who work for me don't have to ask for time off, since they are contract labor and self-employed. But they do. They have the same respect for me and my needs as I have for them. We are a team. They know I am flexible and that I allow them to have their own mind and I expect input on the jobs that we do. I trust them.

Now, think about what job in corporate America will allow you to make your own decisions, take time off when you want, say thank you regularly, buy lunches or dinners, and give you latitude for personal freedom among the demands of daily deadlines and time lines? If you can provide these things, plus a decent wage, you will have provided your help with far more than money.

Many hard working, high salaried employees are miserable in their jobs. Pay is important, but the attitude of the boss and how you are treated make a real difference in someone's life.

This is a give and take world. With the people who work with you, you have to give twice as much as you take. You will never lack hardworking loyal help.

Commercial vs. Residential

Around my 3rd year in business, it became attractive to start doing commercial work. I was being asked to bid on larger scale jobs and I admit it was sexy. I was excited to get into it. I had been running residential services for so long that I was excited about the larger scale jobs, along with the larger scale pay that came with them. I was excited to be working for a business instead of a homeowner.

Homeowners spend hard-earned dollars. Businesses generally have someone who is in charge of spending 'the company's' money. Things looked good and seemed great, but things aren't always what they seem.

Residential work comes faster. Homeowners want a job done and they want it done quickly. A business wants the work done, but it might be a year from now. They just want bids for now. Someone at the company has the job title that says it is his job to do preliminary discovery and determine what they will budget for the project, way in advance. Residential clients want to improve the appearance of their home. Businesses are in no hurry.

Residential work comes with less risk. A smart service provider asks for 50% of the agreed price, prior to starting the job. The balance is due on completion. Commercial jobs are a hurry-up-and-wait game from start to finish. In the beginning it's, "Hurry up and give us a bid." After a month of follow up it's, "We're waiting until next spring to do the work." Next is, "Hurry up and get started." After you finish the job, it is, "Our billing cycle is 45 days."

As a contractor, the waiting game puts you at risk. It is hard to survive long payouts with no deposits. Unless you have plenty of cash in the bank, stay away from commercial accounts. They can drain you financially and they certainly add undue stress. Save yourself for paying jobs that will bring in money consistently.

Warranties and Guarantees

In order to successfully sell your services, you have to provide insurance to the client. People love insurance; they love to know that something they buy is guaranteed. When people buy a car they get a 100K mile warranty. When they buy insurance for their home, they are guaranteed that if a tree falls down and puts a hole through their house, the repairs will be paid for. When they buy a gadget, they often buy an extended warranty plan. All warranties and guarantees are a sales gimmick. That's it and that's all. Don't believe me?

You make the perfect sales presentation and the client is about to buy but stops to ask one last question. "How long is the work warranted?"

You say, "I'm sorry. I don't have a warranty." Will you still have the job when another sales person who eagerly wants the business offers a warranty? I *can guarantee* you won't have that job.

The idea of a warranty or a guarantee is simple. The product or service you sold will last and you will not have to purchase or pay for this service again for X amount of time. The trick is to make sure you present the guarantee and warranty well enough that they feel comfortable buying from you. Make them believe in your warranty and your guarantee and always follow through on any guarantee you promise.

The sales gimmick behind your warranty is your other working sales person in the presentation. He, the warranty, tips the scales toward them spending more money on your product or service than if he isn't offering one.

If your average sale is $1800 and you sell 60 more jobs a year because of your warranty or guarantee, that adds up to $108,000 in increased sales. If your average profit on each job was 65% you earned $70,200 extra by guaranteeing your work. Use it as a tool.

There will be times when you have to go back to a job because something needs fixed or because it didn't last as long as your warranty said it would. Is this going to hurt your profit?

It is something you must evaluate and keep in mind from a cost/risk perspective. If your warranty earned $70,200 in additional profit and 3 jobs didn't make it past your warranty period; you do have to go back and do the job again to meet your customer service standards and customer expectations. Three jobs is not going to hurt you. If you have 3 jobs to redo at an average cost of $630 a job, you will have spent about $1800 to honor your warranty, or about the cost of one job. Using this scenario, it is abundantly clear that the warranty or guarantee was worth selling $108,000 in additional jobs. It is well worth the risk if your product or service doesn't hold up as long as you guarantee. If you are offering a warranty on a service or product that triples these numbers, it will not be worth selling a warranty as you will soon feel as though you are working for free.

In other words, you have to account for redoing jobs and figure them back into your profit and cost model. Make sure your guarantee or warranty makes sense for you and that your guarantee is increasing your sales.

If you don't think a guarantee is necessary for your service and that it may be too risky, that is something to think about and decide based on your particular service or industry.

15

$1000 a day
Wash, Rinse, Repeat

In a job market saturated with hopeful employees searching for a "salary" or a "salary plus benefits," it's easy to lose sight of the opportunities of abundance surrounding us. Making a $1000 a day is not hard. You can do it today. "Sure," you say.

Here are a few examples of ways to do it with little or NO money.

How I started

The hole in the market that I saw,--the opportunity I was tripping over daily--was the decks and fences in my city. They were eyesores more than boundaries of property or privacy. They were nasty, decaying, rotting and reducing the appeal of the neighborhoods. When they weren't that bad, they had a different problem. Each fence was a different color. As you drove down the street, you would see a red fence, a brown fence, then a decaying fence, then a golden yellow fence. Then, Oh My God! a fence painted green.

I saw opportunity.

I first went to the home owners associations. You can find these simply by looking up neighborhoods online and finding the management teams. The builders or even the realtors that sold the homes in the area have all the contact info for the H.O.A.

With business cards in hand, and a lesson or two from the hardware store on how not to beautify a deck or fence--which was the same method the homeowners were using--I brought them pictures. Even though the members of the H.O.A. board drove that very same street daily, it wasn't until I brought photos of the neighborhood fences that they took a second look.

As they looked at the photos, I didn't have to sell what I wanted to do. They saw the problem and somehow knew I was there to offer a solution. At a price, of course.

I showed them pictures of other neighborhoods that didn't have the eyesore problem. I showed them pictures of neighborhoods with preventative measures in place. Homeowners were regulated as to what materials and what colors they were allowed to use.

Call it a higher form of keeping up with the Joneses, or simply not wanting to be second best, or feelings that they were not doing as good a job of keeping up the appearance of the community as other Home Owners Associations, I now had the governing body of over 1000 homes wanting to hear how to fix the problem IMMEDIATELY.

After a sit down with a few of the board members where I showed them the process to remedy the issues, they asked me back to do a full presentation to the entire board.

Pressure Ensues

I was stressed. I had to come with all the materials and a presentation suitable for the board in less than a week. I had to come up with demonstrations, product details, warranties, costs, manufacturers' recommendations, the process and WHY it should be done that way. I had to come up with a time line when I could see it done. Oh, shit.

I calmed myself down and reminded myself I didn't have to do all myself. Delegate!

I contacted 2 paint reps from reputable stain manufacturers and told them my challenge. I was considering using one of two manufacturers for my presentation suggesting the right product to beautify the community. Suddenly I had 2 representatives-- being paid by their employers--working for ME, for FREE.

I told them I needed a presentation of their products, 3 color choices on actual wood that had been aged and also the same colors on new wood. I needed a warranty assuring the H.O.A. board members how long it would last. I needed proof that the process took all the steps recommended by the manufacturers (This allowed me to be the middle man, not the one saying it needed a process based on my opinion.) Soon enough, I had emails loaded with the content I needed to develop the presentation. I had the two reps calling to tell me when I could come by to get the things I asked for. What was their drive? They were paid on volume. How much would they sell if I was successful? I had free employees.

I picked the rep I wanted to use based on who assisted me the most. I asked him to join me at the meeting. This showed several things: number one, it showed the H.O.A that I cared enough to bring in the manufacturer; number two, it showed the H.O.A. that the manufacturer agreed that a decision to hire me would be wise. It was built-in clout and enhanced my reputation.

After the meeting, and a discussion of color options, I was the designated deck and fence eyesore fixer-upper for the entire community.

I was paid an initial $3500 to do the Home Owners Association's wood and any fences not owned by the homeowners.

The HOA sent a letter to all homeowners mandating the colors that were to be used on all fences by a certain date at the expense of the home owners. The letter also suggested they contact the H.O.A.'s chosen service provider (ME) for a quote or to contact them directly if they intended to do it themselves.

The steps involved to fix the issues were above and beyond most of the homeowner's ability and know how. I had an entire community at my fingertips.

I placed signs in the neighborhood that said;

Fence Beautifying
913-933-0060
Deadline 6/01/08

Yes, I reminded them of the deadline.

Phone calls came in faster than I could answer. I signed each client up in person, and collected a 3rd of the price upfront as a deposit. I assured them I would inform the HOA of their intent to conform to the mandatory beautifying of the wood in the neighborhood. I collected $1000s a day.

The rest was easy. I brought the products at a discount from the rep involved in the sales process. I hired labor at $10 an hour and I netted more than $1500 a day for the entire summer from that one marketing effort. This didn't count my other marketing efforts throughout the city.

Another Way--Corner Lot Hunting

When driving around hunting for opportunity around neighborhoods, I first go to the corner lot home owners. People expect the owners of corner lots to keep their home up to higher standards, as they are a focal point of the community. I use this to my advantage.

I go to the door with card in hand and offer them a wonderful deal.

"Hi, my name is Chad Peterson, I own GotWood? a Deck and Fence company specializing in the beautifying of wood. Basically, we give wood a face lift and can take 10 years off of the age of your fence or deck.

The reason I stopped by today at your home specifically, is because you have a corner lot. I would --AT MY COST--make your fence look brand new if I can place a sign in your yard for the entire year showing the neighborhood how beautiful their fence could be if they use me."

The homeowner is thinking, *I am cooking dinner. How fast can I get this guy away from my house? But wait. He said he could make my fence look ten years younger and he will do it at cost. My house will be the benchmark for the neighborhood.*

The next question is always, "How much will it cost?"

"As I said, I will do it at my cost. It is a free way to get your fence looking new and preserved. All I ask is that you keep my sign in your yard all year long. I can give you my costs if I walk your fence and measure the amount of product I will use. Are you interested?"

I get a lot more yes's than no's in this scenario.

I figure my costs at RETAIL price, of course. If I charge $52 a gallon, but can buy it through my rep for $22, I make money on the deal.

Next, I figure out my labor costs. I am going to pay $12 an hour and it will take 16 hours from start to finish. My cost is roughly $200 in labor and $230 in product including prep chemicals, stain, etc. So my hard cost combined is $430, plus $430 for my own labor.

Normally, this fence I would have cost the homeowner $1580, or just under $1600 to sell it. When I show them a savings of $720, if they say yes, I will not making a killing, but I will make $430 and have a home to use as a bill board all year long. The advertisement will make the neighbors want the same beautiful fence. My total cost on that job is $430 and I ask for that amount as a deposit so I can pay for "materials", in all actuality the client already paid for all of my labor and material and I have free advertising for the entire year. Plus I earned a profit; quite a clever way to get paid for advertising. I can usually close 3 corner lots in a day.

Another Way: Work for others--kind of.

Look around. Find painters, window companies, deck companies, cleaning companies, roofers, remodelers, etc. Tell them you want to market their services. Do you think they would be interested in a free employee marketing their services? Yes, indeed.

Ask them what they do, how they bid them, what income they shoot for with certain projects. Get any promotional material, handouts, etc., that they have. Ask them for sales points and how they present their services. Basically, have them train you to sell their products. This is espionage in its easiest form.

So, what just happened? A company taught you how to look at a project or service, how to bid it, what to look out for, how much it costs to do it and how much they want to charge for the service. Plus they gave you print and promotional material. What else do you need to know to sell for your own company now that you have the knowledge?

Or do the honorable thing and go to those very same companies and tell them you are in marketing. Tell them you want to market their services. They teach you, train you, and perhaps even endear themselves to you as an asset. You then have a team around you training you, grooming you to sell and imparting their knowledge to you.

The first thing you need to know is their pricing. If that company charges $2500 for a particular style house to be painted, you know anything above that is yours. Never work for only the amount you add to the price. Make sure you earn at least 10% of the gross price tag.

Let's say you place ads on craigslist, you place fliers, you post on face book, you hand out cards, network at your networking meeting, or buy and place signs and handle the inbound call volume and sell house painting.

So you sell painting for that particular style house for $3100 and earn a percentage of the original $2500. Your net earnings would be $600 per home.

In short, you learned all they know about painting homes, you are given inside secrets of the trade and how to bid. You now market a service that you don't have any equipment to do, and you have marked the service up a touch and made income from the painting company, essentially as a free employee off of the payroll, marketing their services at no charge to them. This is a TRIPLE WIN.

On the other hand, let's say you do the less than honorable thing and learn the secrets and do it yourself. In this case, you would charge the $3100, run ghost ads on craigslist and have a few hundred painters who not only have the equipment, but who also know how to paint houses begging for your business. It will take 4 days with 2 men to paint the home. You may have $750 in labor, maybe $650 in paint and materials. Your total profit is $1700.

If you want to make $100,000 a year, you have to do this 60 times a year or 5 homes a month.

I speak from experience; this is easy to do if you follow these steps.

16

Life Style Design

It's more than a catchy buzz phrase. It's more like a wake-up call.

If you are unfamiliar with the term Lifestyle Design, don't expect a grandiose answer because the answer is simply **work to live rather than live to work**.

 Another way of thinking about lifestyle design is reducing the amount of time and effort you spend working and increasing the time and effort spent doing things you enjoy. I don't mean eliminating overtime or not working on weekends. I mean drastically increasing your time away from work to improve the quality of your life. I mean time to enjoy doing the things you love to do.

The term Lifestyle Design has been a buzz word used a lot over the last ten years. The deafening truth is that "Retirement has failed." Work a lot while you're young and retire later has failed completely.

If you work your mind and back to death and suffer from health problems at the age of 65, only to **hopefully** retire, doesn't that sound awful and downright depressing? It most certainly is and yet most don't think about a better or faster route to enjoying life because most are chasing the normal route their mothers and fathers took. Perhaps their own peers are doing it now.

But many "out there" are living wonderful lives full of abundance and leisure time without the burden of work and the demanding requirements of working. You may not be yet, but that life is what we are going to focus on.

The path to success can seem long. The struggle is a winding road and success comes with many obstacles. There are many things that can go wrong and critical decisions to be made in order to stay on track. Market changes, company downsizing and technological advances reduce the number of jobs and some are completely eliminated. What if you get ill or hurt? Many things can add challenges to life but I personally can't think of anything more complicated, more hopeless than our outdated model of retirement. Work all your life so that one day you can relax.

The first problem with that model is that sometimes, one day never comes. Do you plan to live forever? If at 65, you are still on the right side of the soil and carrying on, you **might** be able to live your dreams. *If* you have done all the necessary work and responsibly set aside enough to live your dreams. Have you accomplished all you wanted to accomplish so that at the old age of 65, you can sit back and relax?

I am currently 34 years old and from collegiate wrestling, collegiate Rugby, being rowdy all my life, and adding in a few accidents and injuries; I have aches and pains that I don't sense will go away as I get older. I doubt I'll be lighting the world on fire when I retire.

If I don't go trek those mountains now, perhaps I never will. If I don't dive the Great Barrier Reef now, I won't be able to later. If I don't take that cross country motorcycle ride north to south and east to west to all the national parks, I may never do it. Chances are I won't if I don't do it now.

The New Face of Retirement

The cat is out of the bag. Retirement isn't what it was supposed to be.

So what does it look like now? The boom of the internet, technological advancements and availability to the market has created a culture of doers and vagabonds. They are the "lifestyle design masters."

The idea is simple. Don't defer living and put it off until later. Instead, design your life around doing what you love. Create a career that enables you to reduce the time spent working so you can spend more time living.

Perhaps world travel is your thing. Perhaps you want to spend more time with family. Maybe you have hobbies you love or just value leisure time and the opportunity to do a wide variety of things. Or you just might not like being a slave to the system.

What do you do for a living? Are you passionate about it? Does it serve you emotionally and spiritually? Do you crave more work or do you resist your job like the burden it is?

Too many options exist for anyone who is fed up with working themselves to death to continue doing it. Why? For a chance to *hopefully* relax one day?

So many options exist that you could quit your job immediately and create the life you want by following the steps I'm showing you here. I've done it. I've shown others how to do it. I know you can do it, too, if you take the right steps.

If you want to take the steps toward personal freedom and design a lifestyle tailored just for you, you must set a dead line for yourself. How much longer are you willing to settle for your current life? How long will you give yourself before you say "enough is enough?" Once you decide when your deadline of leaving your J.O.B. is, follow the D.E.A.D.L.I.N.E acronym as you step off your J.O.B. rock.

D-Decide

Decide to live the life you want rather than the life you have subconsciously accepted. If your life isn't what you think it should be, why live that life another day? Why haven't you DECIDED enough is enough? 80% of life is about decision making. The other 20% nit-picking details we convince ourselves are important before we can take action. The truth is that we don't need to know the details before we do something. The details will present themselves once you make a decision.

Pretend you are about to pack the car and take a trip to Florida with your family or friends. It dawns on you that the headlights only reveal 150 feet of the road ahead and you are about to drive 2500 miles to go to the beach. How will you get there if your headlights reveal 150 feet in front of you?

You realized that as you drive, the further you go, the further you will see. The headlights will illuminate the road ahead all the way to your destination, 150 feet at a time.

This is life and this is how life works. You didn't know how to walk, tie your shoes or play sports but that didn't stop you from learning. You didn't always know what was around the next corner, but that didn't stop you from turning the corner to find out. The answers always come, it's the universe's way of giving you what you need when you need it.

We get too caught up worrying about HOW we will do something and we often don't make the DECISION towards our goals or to make a change because we think we have to know all the answers before we decide. Once you decide you have had too much pain from the life you are living and decide you are willing to do whatever it takes to live the life you want, you have decided…the rest is easy.

Deciding to live your life the way you see it is empowering. It prevents excuses. It stops "one day" thinking. It liberates and allows change and lets good things come into your life. Magic exists for those who dedicate themselves to exploring possibilities. That leads to limitless thinking and is usually the result of knowing when enough is enough.

The pain far outweighs the pleasure of living a lack luster, circumstances ran life. You have the power within to create the life you desire. You just have to decide.

E-Eliminate

You can't reach for anything new if your hands are full of yesterday's junk. (I wish I knew who said that. I'd give him or her credit.)

To make way for the new, we have to get rid of the old. Elimination is the key to allowing new or different things to present themselves to you.

Are you over worked and under paid? *Eliminate.* Are you hurting inside because nothing about your job makes you feel good? *Eliminate.* Do you work weekends and over time, trying to get ahead? *Eliminate.* Do life's demands prevent you from taking care of yourself? *Eliminate.* Do you run 100 MPH all day, every day to get everything done? *Eliminate.* Whatever is not necessary you must eliminate.

Time wasting meetings, grueling long hours, endless errands and life tasks consume time that could be better spent taking action toward building the life you dream of. *Eliminate* it all. Stop anything that is not getting you closer to the life you want.

This isn't time management refined. This is flat out refusal to continue activities that fail to get you the results you want. Spend your time on high output and high leveraging tasks.

I boldly tell those around me what I don't want to do if it gets in the way of doing what makes me very productive. For instance, my assistant does things and asks if the way it was done is what I had in mind. While seemingly the order of things, she is very good at what she does. I trust her. I am intently focused on what I need to do, at what I am good at. Rather than checking, rechecking, and God forbid, managing the people around me, I delegate what I am not good at and focus on what I do extremely well. Rather than trying to fix shortcomings or inadequacies, maximize your talents and work around your weaknesses. Eliminate all that does not serve you. Delegate at all costs. Surround yourself with people who compliment your talents and reduce your weaknesses.

Eliminate mindless, time wasting activities

I haven't had cable TV in over a decade. When I am in a home where TV is "what they do," I wonder how I could do all the things I do if I did what they do? Then I wonder what are they NOT doing? Don't they have dreams? What would they do if they weren't too busy watching TV?

The world is full of people busy with mindless activities, zoning out their passions and dreams. Don't be one of them. Live life rather letting it slide by while you are watching actors, athletes, and public figures live their dreams. Lose the social media addiction Facebook has to be the biggest time waster and mind numbing activity of the 21st century.

Eliminate misguided focus. For instance, your favorite wonderful singer and songwriter suddenly announces his whacky political views and commits career suicide. The guy had genius written all over him. Why the distraction? Stick with what you do well and do it. Don't let your focus blur and lose momentum.

A-Action

Take action. There's no time better than the present. Take action, but don't take ordinary action. Take MASSIVE action.

What does massive action look like? I will use myself as an example. I didn't have the money for the equipment needed to start my own mud jacking company, and I refuse to borrow money, but I saw the need in the market. I knew customers were seeking the service and I wanted to own a company that provided it. It is a very high profit margin service and there is vast need across the country with few providers.

I eliminated all the distractions, including my own negative self talk. I knew I was going to do it. With no training, no equipment, no tools, and not even a name picked out, I took the massive action and made 150 dials a day to call local contractors and businesses to see if they had a need to sell Mud Jacking. Most said that they had customers asking them all the time but they didn't offer it. I asked them if I could I sit down with them and give them a quote?

I booked 3 large accounts totaling $23,000 in revenue before I even had the equipment or the knowledge.

 Within a month I had 27 websites up under the name of Boss Mud jacking and a bunch of DBAs that allowed me complete market penetration under many different names. That aided in market exposure. I knew I was going to do it; though I knew little about it. I decided.

I eliminated.

I applied massive action.

With usual fashion, I placed 1000's of my billboards across the city; I contacted everyone in the market who might need to sell or use my service. Day and night, I penetrated and saturated the market.

I am now the largest Mud Jacking Company in the Midwest and have more websites and market exposure than any company out there. I offer franchises across the country and have quickly became nationwide.

Compare that to my competition. They are operating day to day, thinking inside the box. If we don't live in a box and don't think inside a box and allow ourselves to be completely unrealistic, we often get unrealistic results.

Be unrealistic if you want to be successful. We all know our share of unrealistic people. Aren't they the ones who soar above, beyond normalcy, living great lives? You can too. Take massive action.

D- Discover and Duplicate

In creating the life you want, find 3 things that aid in your success. The 3 things that work for you must first be Discovered. Then you must Duplicate those 3 things, again and again and again with massive action.

Discover your own path and the steps you need to take and along the way. Find things that work for you. Years ago when cell technology was taking off and everyone was getting their first cell phones, I saw that having my name and service number all over the city would be a leg up on the competition. I couldn't afford bill boards or expensive yellow page ads, but I imagined my name being on political-type yard signs all over the city. My first week, I answered 75 phone calls requesting bids. I had discovered one of the 3 things that work for me.

I duplicated this time and time again and took massive action to do it relentlessly. I knew that I had a new problem on my hands though. How was I going to handle all of the business? I didn't let it slow me down and discovered another of my 3 important ingredients and I duplicated it with massive action. I had more calls than I could handle. I didn't decide that I had plenty of calls and pull back on marketing. I was out every night, marketing, doing everything I could to duplicate the success. I was tenacious about it.

The second ingredient of my 3 was my presentation and my branding appeal. I knew that if I showed up to a job and looked the part, had the carbonless copies of my agreements, my business cards looking top notch and my sales delivery flawless; I had the business. No one stood a chance at getting the business. Still today I know deep in my heart that if my competitors are competing against me directly in a sale, they have lost before they even try.

The 3rd ingredient of my success was my ability to find good help readily available at all times. If I did the 1st ingredient to perfection, and my second ingredient was flawless, if I didn't have the help I needed I would be sunk, dead in my tracks. I began to post ads on craigslist. I call them "ghost ads". These ads are for anything and everything that I do and don't offer in my business. I have posted help wanted ads for carpenters, painters, stucco workers, brick layers, landscapers, cleaners, tree removal services, concrete workers, etc. I have placed 100s of 'seeking tradesman' ads and I never respond to the replies. I make sure that the applicant for the supposed job replies with a resume, a phone number and a good email for me to contact them. I use a Gmail account so that the data is never lost and always available to me through my phone at an instant. When someone asks me, "Do you do stucco?" "Why, yes I do." is my answer. "Do you paint houses?" "Why, yes I do. We are the best in the city." "Do you make women's underwear?" "That's our specialty." Whatever it is you want to do and things you don't want to do, find others that DO. Have them available at a click of a button in your email as a contact and voila you have officially entered the market as a 'do it all' business.

L-Leverage

Whether you are lifting something heavy and need to squat to get beneath it for leverage or you are trying to open a pickle jar and have to get your shoulder into it to pop that top off, leveraging all your resources and any around you maximizes your efforts.

Leverage says that two is better than one, that three is better than two. Leverage is taking all of your skills, talents, resources, tools and tricks to accomplish what you want to accomplish.

An old proverb says that if you give a man a long enough lever, he can move the world.

I have seen it happen time and time again. If you have a goal in mind, it's hard to achieve it single handedly. If it was that easy, it wouldn't be a goal, would it? Getting to your goals takes leverage.

Look at your current circumstance. Where do you want to be 6 months from now? A year? Two years? How much business do you want? Get beneath that goal, use every amount of leverage you have. Now lift. Ask for help. Get assistance. Pay for coaching. Use any talent you possess. Give it all you've got. Leverage to success.

Here is an example: I know that I am good at marketing, branding, selling, and being resourceful at getting things done. It's not only my specialty, but what I was born to do. In order to leverage those skills, I have to make sure my team around me knows full well what my strengths are but more importantly my weaknesses. My assistant knows what I do and don't want to do, and she removes the things I don't want to deal with daily; leaving me room to do what I am good at. This is leverage. While she is handling things that would otherwise reduce my efficiency, I am leveraging my skills. Another example, I am not into Facebook or social media in general, nor am I motivated to do online marketing through networking, tweeting, and cultivating an audience. I want nothing to do with website development or maximizing traffic. I had Hippodaddy.com step in and they have done a wonderful job. Hippo Daddy prides themselves' on being proactive with their clients. By making adjustments, establishing creative marketing strategies and always pushing the envelope in your online marketing campaign, Hippo Daddy will do whatever it takes to maximize your online exposure. They truly believe that the only measure of their success is that of their clients… and they work hard to earn it. Having them in my corner, they are leveraging what I do out in the field maximizing my efforts and reducing time spent on tasks not suitable for me.

I-Identify

Identify what you want. This one is easy, right? You want a million dollars. You want a snazzy, cool car. No. It isn't that simple.

Be very, very clear about what you want and be very, very specific. Make no mistake; if you are not clear about what you want, you won't get it. I promise that.

You must be implicitly clear about what you want and not worry about the HOW you will get it. Once you decide what you want, you will manifest it in your life as you take steps towards your goals.

The law of attraction and the law of manifestation are laws you must abide by.

If you say you will make 200K next year but don't know if you'll get it or if you'll receive it, you won't believe you can.

Once you identify what you very specifically want, you have nothing left to do but keep your mind in the state that will help you get it. It's just that simple.

N-Navigate Gently

You. Are. Not. In. Control.

You and I are merely ships on a rough sea that is totally out of control. We can make slight adjustments, we can make navigational turns, but the turns are slight and they are less effective than we would like. In order to navigate to success, we have to be centered and peaceful. We have to be content in our heart and in tune with what our instincts tell us.

If you navigate your ship with large perilous turns, you will make many more mistakes than if you make minor adjustments. The universe gives you what you need to accomplish the wishes you've identified. Small changes along the way let things unfold with the flow, as they should. Minor changes are blessings in disguise.

When you sense that things aren't going exactly the way you thought they would, realize that this is normal. But think about it. Things will come to you as you think about what you want and take massive action to get there. Creative solutions to problems will occur to you. But you must be able to let things happen so you don't get in your own way.

Allow things to navigate naturally. Make minor changes along the way. You may very well end up with different results than you originally intended, but often they are much, much bigger and better than you ever imagined.

E-Envision

The Bible says: Where there is no vision, the people perish.

Nothing happens without envisioning. All things are created by someone thinking, 'What if...' I imagine Edison 'saw' the light bulb long before he made one and then made one work. If he didn't see something, how would he have even known where to start?

You must see something in your mind before you can believe it can come true.

Envisioning is an important step in finding success. It brings to life something that isn't real. Once you can see it, it starts to feel real. The more you can see it, the more real it feels. Results will begin to manifest in your life.

Once clarity begins to show itself, you will see hints and be prompted take more action as more answers are revealed to you in your journey of manifesting your dreams.

The mind can't create what it cannot imagine.

You begin the process by envisioning what your success looks like, in color, with details, with price tags.

What does it look like?

How does it feel?

Think about what you want and imagine it time and time again until it comes your way. It works, every time.

17

Time to Get Started

Emotions and Goals

I am not Michael Jordan. I am not Donald Trump. I am not Steven Spielberg. Why? Because I didn't have the emotional drive to propel me to do what they did. They are at the top of the food chain in their various careers because they had a passionate emotion about what they did and turned it into a living.

They had emotional reasons behind their goals. It is what drove them.

Michael Jordan imagined and felt what it would be like to win. His emotional drive guided his team to victory time and time again. But he saw it before it ever even happened.

Donald Trump felt the art of the deal long before he made his first million. Billions of dollars later, he still feels the emotional pull towards those deals.

Steven Spielberg envisioned making movies and felt what it was like to be a great film maker long before he made one that anyone saw. The emotion behind his dreams made his dream come true.

They all knew what they wanted; they felt what it was like to have it before they became mega successful.

Their dreams came true because they passionately and emotionally charged their dreams and passionately and emotionally did what it took to turn them into reality.

You must do the same if you want to achieve your own kind of greatness.

A dream without emotional passion behind it is nothing. When thinking of your dreams and aspirations, think of the reasons and the emotions behind those dreams and aspirations.

We're going to explore your dreams and passions now.

For the following exercises, you will need a notebook and a pen. These answers will be written in the notebook of your choice so they are easily accessible to you at any given time.

Use it as your reference for your goals and the reasons why these goals are so important to you. Answer them as honestly as you can, without limitation.

The world puts limitations on us, our peers and those we surround ourselves with have what is possible for you in their minds. They think they know what is not possible for you, but that reality is only their reality. You are different. You know deep inside that being "realistic" is a self imposed limitation. Those limitations thwart the success waiting around the corner for you. You are the one who will decide not to live in "reality" pressed upon you. Rather you will soar above the red tape and the limitations both set by others and more importantly yourself, limitation imposed by you. On you.

In all likelihood, you are the most negative force keeping you from your dreams and reaching your goals.

Now, step out of your own way and allow greatness to unfold before you by defining what you want, why, and what timeline you will adhere to in order to get there. Set a definitive timeline. No limitations. No excuses.

Let's begin.

Discovery Questions

How many hours do you work in one year?
Is that how many hours you want to work each year?

What time do you get your day started?

What time do you get home?

Do you have time to spare in your days or is every moment of your day predictable with one task after another after another until the day runs out?

How much money do you make an hour?

How much do you make a year?

Do you making as much money as you would like to make?

Is your lifestyle what you want it to be now?

Is the home you live in your dream home?

Are you passionate about what you do for a living?

Are you investing for retirement?

Do you have a long term plan for retirement with plenty of money to spare now and then?

Now, really look at your answers.

Look at them closely and let the reality of today sink in. Make sure your answers are as honest as they can be and honestly ask yourself if you are happy.

Are you happy now? Are you happy with your answers so far?

If you are not happy, so why are you living in the above reality? Who, if anyone, can make the changes to make your answers ones that will make you happy? Are you waiting for your ship to come in? Are you waiting for the dreams and happiness to come your way by accident? As you trudge through your Mondays through Fridays, working for someone else's dreams, do you expect your ship to float in?

The odds of your dreams coming true while you work for someone else are 1 in the hundreds of millions. So why are you working for someone else and trading in your dreams for someone else's? The answer is fear. Fear of failure. Fear of not knowing how to do it. Fear of falling flat on your face. Fear of possible financial mistakes.

Being self employed is never easy, but unless you take charge of your own life and the responsibility that comes with it, you will never reach your goals. You will not reach your career goals. You will not reach your goals of how you want to spend your valuable time. And you will not reach your financial goals.

So now let's define those goals so we can start eliminating the fears and getting rid of the limitations you put on yourself.

Close your eyes and imagine the life you want. Do not put any limitations on what you envision. None. If you see yourself sitting on a beach wearing linen with umbrellas in your drink, we will get you there. Nothing is impossible. Nothing.

Sit and dream. Sit and imagine what your life should and could look like. Think of what you want. Think about what you want to give and share with others. Now, no matter how long it takes, imagine what your life would be if your dreams came true. What it would look like? How much money would you earn? How much would you have in the bank? What kind of house would you live in? What car would be in the drive? Envision it all coming true.

Now write out what those dreams looked like. This is your book, your journal. No one will read it but you, so write it honestly and without hesitation. Make it detailed. Make it graphic. Write out your dream without holding anything back.

Now that you see what your life would look like if you were living your dreams, let's get specific and put it all in order. Turn the page in your notebook and answer these questions now.

How many hours a week would you like to work? Why?

How much money would you like to make a year? Why?

What emotion does making this amount of money give you?

How much time would you like to have each week to spend as you want?

Why?

What emotion do you feel about your free time?

Where would you like to live?

Why?

What emotion does living where you want to live give you?

With more time each week, how will you use it to take better care of yourself?

Why?

What emotion does being healthier and in better shape give you?

If you could go anywhere and see anything, what would it be?

Are you willing to work for both money and freedom for yourself? Why?

What emotion does seeing all you want to see and doing all you want to do in life give you?

How would those around you benefit from your higher income and free time?

Why?

What emotion do you feel knowing you can offer those around you a better life?

How much money do you need for retirement?

Why?

What emotion does it give you to know that you have money to live well now and in retirement?

Now let's take some time to analyze.

So far, what is becoming the most common reason why you want what you do?

What reason is the most notable and significant? What emotion drives you to reach your goals? What emotion is the most common in your answers?

The emotion is that is the most common is the one that will drive you to reach your goals. Let that driving emotion be your fire in the belly, the steam behind the train when your fear makes you cautious to take that next step, when those around you, or your own small voice warns you that you are extending beyond your abilities. That emotion will push you to the end—if you let it. Remember that emotion. Treasure that feeling and let it immerse you when you think of why you want to reach these goals. This is the recipe for your success.

Timeline

Your timeline is very important. It will map out the steps you must take and will also be a reference point and a progress report. You must check your progress against your timeline, every now and then. Evaluate whether you are accomplishing what you set out to accomplish. Your time line must start with today. "One day" never comes. Let others say one day. You start today. Today make progress by taking one giant step towards something you want. Today, write out 10 things you need to do immediately to get headed in the right direction. Today, set a deadline for getting all 10 things done, make a check list. When every item is complete, write down another 10 things and attack it with the same vigor you did your first ten.

Good luck. Let us help when we can. We would love to hear about your success. Visit our website at: www.bluetowhite.com and keep us posted on our forum page and be sure to sign up to receive industry news and blogs directly from the site by signing up at http://bluetowhite.wordpress.com

Appendix

The following agreements or contracts are yours to use as an example. Use these as a starting point; feel free to use language directly from the documents. The agreements should be written to protect you.

As you will see, the backs of the agreements itemize how I conduct my relationship with clients. I make sure the expectations are set from a scheduling standpoint, getting paid, and of course, their expectation of what the final product will be.

I say what I will do for them and set rules or guidelines as to what they need to do in order for me to be effective at meeting their needs and expectations. These documents clarify the transaction from start to finish. Before work starts, I make sure each client signs the agreements, and that all aspects of the transaction have been discussed.

In creating your own documents, write them exactly the way you want them. Don't be afraid to tell the clients not to call about scheduling; don't be afraid to address penalties if they don't pay on time; define your terms and it will ensure a smooth transaction. Your agreements should take a lot of the headaches out of managing your business.

If you have questions, we are here: www.bluetowhite.com.

PETERSON CONSTRUCTION & ROOFING

913 933- 0060

AGREEMENT

This agreement is ☐ is not ☐ Subject to Insurance Company Approval

Name _____   Date _____

Address _____   City/ State _____

Billing Address _____   City/ State _____

Home # _____ Work # _____   Email _____

Specifications

☑ Grade of Shingle
☑ Style of Shingle
☑ Color of Shingle
☑ Ridge Material (Matching)
☑ Valley (Matching)
☑ Vents (Matching)   Power Vent Y N
☑ Plumbing Stacks (Matching)
☑ Metal Edging   per code
☑ Tear Off   Y N   Layers   All
☑ Felt   per code
☑ Pitch   Stories
☑ Remove trash from roof, gutters and yard
☑ Protect landscaping (where applicable)
☑ Roll yard and driveway with magnetic roller
☑ Furnish Permit

Special Instructions

Delivery Instructions

I/ We the owners of the premises at the above address offer to contract with Peterson Construction and Roofing to furnish, deliver and arrange for installation of all materials necessary to improve the premises. Homeowner acknowledges Peterson Construction and Roofing as 'general contractor' and as such will be entitled to 10%overhead and 10%profit as allowed by insurance industry standards.
Note to Insurance/ Mortgage Company: I hereby authorize the insurance and mortgage company below to make any checks jointly.
Terms: This agreement does not obligate the homeowner or contractor in any way unless approved by the insurance company and accepted by Peterson Construction and Roofing. When Price Agreeable is determined, it shall become the final contract price indicated in the payment section, including supplements authorized by insurance. The homeowner authorizes Peterson Construction and Roofing to obtain labor and materials in accordance with the Price Agreeable and the specifications set out herein and on the reverse side to accomplish the replacement or repair.

Payment Section	By: _____
Total Contract Amount (+ Supplements)	By: _____
$_____	Accepted by homeowner on Date: ____/ ____/ _____
Down Payment $_____	
Date ____/ ____/ _____	

Insurance Company	
Claim #	
Mortgage Company	
Acct. #	
Address	
City/ State/ Zip	
Phone #	
Field Supervisor	
Management Approval	

Balance Due on Completion

_____ + Supplements

223

CHAD PETERSON

Both sides of this document, including the terms and conditions below, and any agreement execute in writing, pursuant thereto, between Peterson Construction and Roofing (the Company) and the Propter owner's representative(s) hereby referred to as the 'customer' are subject to the laws in effect in the State in which it has been signed and executed.

ANY REPRESENTATION, STATEMENTS, OR OTHER COMMUNICATIONS NOT WRITTEN IN THIS CONTRACT, OR MADE IN WRITING PURSUANT THERETO, ARE AGREED TO BE INVALID, AND NOT RELIED ON BY EITHER PARTY AND, DO NOT SURVICE THE EXECUTION OF THIS CONTRACT.

1. This contract is subject to credit and pricing approval of the management of the company.
2. Payment is due for materials when delivered. Payment is due for the remainder of the contract with the completion of each individual trade, including applicable overhead and profit, such as: Roofing, Siding & Trim, Gutters, Awnings and Carports, Interior Repairs, Punch List. We will issue a Certificate of Substantial Completion when we have completed the scope of the contract. In the event a final inspection is required before the Customer chooses to pay, the Customer shall agree to pay the total balance due, less than 10% as hold-back until the final inspection and any subsequent punch list is completed.
3. Should default be made in payment of this contract, a lien will be placed on the property and charges will be added from the date of substantial completion at the maximum allowed by law. If placed in the hands of an attorney for collection, all attorney and legal fees will be paid by the Customer.
4. The Company and the Customer agree to settle all disputes through the American Arbitration Association.
5. The full amount of all moneys as specified by an agreed price, or as specified by "Full Scope of Insurance Proceeds" does not include any extras such as carpentry repairs, or any other repairs not covered not specified, and not covered by the "Full Scope of Insurance Proceeds," that is necessary to complete the repair process as required by the local building codes and building officials, or to satisfy cosmetically, the Customer.
6. If the "Customer" chooses not to pay for a part of the scope of the contract, an individual line item, or a trade, the Customer releases the Company of its obligations for the performance of that component with regard to the integrity of the building system as a whole.
7. The company is not responsible for damage below the roof due to leaks caused by excessive wind greater than 55 mph, ice, or hail at any time during construction process, or the warranty period.
8. The company is not responsible for slight scratching and denting of gutters, oil droplets in driveways, hairline fractures in concrete, flowers or minor broken branches on plans and shrubbery.
9. This contract cannot be cancelled at any time prior to midnight of the third business day after the date of this agreement.
10. This contract cannot be cancelled once negotiations begin with your insurance, and or once material has been delivered to the customer's job site without written mutual agreement of both parties.
11. If this contract is cancelled by the customer later than three (3) days from execution, Customer agrees to pay the company 25% of the contract price for: 1) Consulting Services Rendered, or 2) Liquidateing fees. If materials have to be returned due to this cancellation, the Customer agrees to pay an additional fee of 10% for re-stocking.
12. The Company reserves the right to supplement Insurance Company for increases in the "Full Scope of Work" and, or, document price increases. Customer agrees to allow these supplements to be paid directly to the Company.
13. All excess materials remain the property of the Company.
14. "Full Scope of Insurance Proceeds shall be defined as the full price of repairs and replacements allowed by the Insurance Company.
15. If any provisions of the contract should be held invalid or unenforceable, the validity and enforceability of the remaining provisions shall not be affected thereby.

Warranty

OUR STANDARD WORKMANSHIP WARRANTY IS FOR TWO (5) YEARS. IN ADDITION, WE WILL PROVIDE A FREE SERVICE CALL FOR INSPECTION FOR AS LONG AS YOU OWN THE PROPERTY. WE WILL PROVIDE YOU A WRITTEN WARRANTY UPON RECEIVING YOUR PAYMENT IN FULL FOR THIS CONTRACT. COPIES ARE AVAIABLE FOR YOUR REVIEW.

Please make checks payable to Peterson Construction and Roofing. No cash is to be paid in accordance with this contract.

BOSS MUD JACKING
KANSAS CITY'S LEADING MUD JACKING COMPANY

(816) 301-6261
Warranted and Guaranteed
www.bossmudjacking.com

Job#:_____   Date_____/_____/_____
Name: _____
Address: _____

Phone: _____ Cell: _____ Email: _____

2 Year Guarantee

Total:

I,_____ have read and agree to all aspects of the agreement (including back) of contract. I hereby Contract Boss Mudjacking to_____ for the price of $_____ All covenants binding contractually. The contract price is valid for Eight (8) days from the date of agreement.

Date of Agreement:_____/_____/_____

Customer Signature_____ Print:_____

Associate Signature _____ Print:_____

1. Boss Mudjacking is a production company working around scheduling, weather, soil conditions and, of course, demand. We service customers in a timely fashion but Boss MudJacking cannot guarantee exact dates of when the work will be started or completed. If you are concerned that we have not yet arrived to perform the work do not call, we are in the field and work as fast as we can. Your business is very important to us and our livelihood; it is our main goal to get your work completed.

2. Boss MudJacking warranties all work performed for 2 years from the date of this agreement.

3. Customer acknowledges that holes will be drilled to complete the job and will be filled with concrete after we are done raising the concrete.

4. Customer agrees that Boss MudJacking cannot guarantee that cracking will not occur. MudJacking by its nature is based on lifting concrete and cracking can occur. Boss MudJacking is not responsible for any cracking that may occur during the lifting process.

5. Boss Mudjacking requires $1/3^{rd}$ of the total price of the repair upfront in order to be put on our schedule. This assures that you have in fact hired us, and pays for the materials that we are placing under your concrete.

6. Unless otherwise noted, Boss Mudjacking estimates are for use of high quality, long lasting and durable mixture of Sand, Cement, Sodium Bentonite, and water. This turns into a 1500 PSI material and should solve any further washout issues in the future, eliminating further need of Mud Jacking services.

7. Boss Mudjacking often leaves bills on doors or emails the final bill, customer agrees to pay the day the work is complete. If we are unable to meet for payment the day the work is complete customer agrees to send the payment the following day via mail **to 1317 Union Kansas City, Missouri 64101. Make all checks payable to Peterson Construction.** A $25 per day late fee will be added each day after 3 days of not receiving final payment.

8. Customer agrees to contact Chad Peterson at his direct cell number if there are any issues prior to complaining on the web, to the BBB, or otherwise. All issues can be handled and customer service is guaranteed by calling 913-207-5895 to reach Chad Peterson, the owner, directly.

9. Customer agrees to allow Boss MudJacking to place a sign in yard the day we agree to do work for you, and up to 30 days after completion of the work.

Customer Service Guarantee

Like Us On **f**
facebook

http://www.facebook.com/bossmudjacking

SERVICE CONTRACT

Job#:_____   Date_____/_____/_____

Name: _____

Address: _____

_____

Phone: _____ Cell: _____ Email: _____

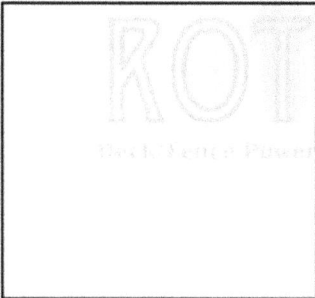

Prep Chemicals.	$_____
Repair Work.	$_____
Power washing.	$_____
Application	$_____
Product:_____	
Final Price:	$_____
Special Instruction:	

_____

I,_____ have Read and agree to all aspects of the agreement on back of contract. I hereby Contract Rot Knot to _____ for the price of $_____ All covenants binding contractually. The contract price is valid for Eight (8) days from the date of agreement.

Date of Agreement:_____/_____/_____

Customer Signature_____ Print:_____

Associate Signature _____ Print:_____

1. Rot Knot is a production company working around scheduling, weather, and _____.
   Rot Knot Cannot guarantee exact dates of when deck or fence will be worked on. If
   Customer is concerned Rot Knot has not arrived to perform the work do not call, we are
   in the field and work as fast as we can.

2. Rot Knot does not guarantee a brand new deck/fence from the work being performed.
   Age and condition of deck determines results.

3. Customer acknowledges not all stain will be removed after power wash and prep.

4. Customer is responsible for removal of items attached to the deck or a charge of $50.00
   above contract agreement

5. Customer will be contacted day Prior to the completion of the job. Payment in full is due
   and payable the day the job is completion, a $20 per day late fee will be charged for
   each per day past the job completion date until paid in full.

6. Customer is responsible for cleanliness of deck after Rot Knot power washes (cleans)
   Deck/house unless due to weather.

7. After application of stain no contact with deck or fence for 72hrs. (Pets, furniture,
   humans, etc.)

8. If customer wants to change color it must be done within 48hrs of contract being signed.

9. Rot Knot will leave contractor's sign from date of agreement until date of completion in
   front yard for advertising purposes.

10. If problems, concerns, or complaints occur. Rot Knot guarantees our work. The Initial
    contract amount in full prior to scheduling any additional work or repairs.

11. Contract of services to be performed are legal binding, regardless of customer service
    issues, cancelling or un-satisfaction, you must pay contracted amount. Rot Knot
    guarantees work we must guarantee payment. Cancellation of any signed contract will
    result in a $200.00 Cancellation fee.

ABOUT THE AUTHOR

Chad Peterson has operated more than 10 businesses that have earned over 20 million in revenue over a short span of years. He has taught and inspired 100s of others to create six figure incomes in service related industries with his guerilla marketing techniques. His successful strategies redefine the modern Blue Collar worker and afford him freedom and he travels the world, spending most of his winters in locales such as Belize, Honduras, and Panama.

www.ingramcontent.com/pod-product-compliance
Lightning Source LLC
Chambersburg PA
CBHW060014210326
41520CB00009B/879